OTHER BOOKS BY MIE PUBLISHING

Find Anyone Fast

Secrets of Finding Unclaimed Money

How to Locate Anyone Who Is or Has Been in the Military

Check 'Em Out Series

Checking Out Lawyers

by Don Ray

MIE PUBLISHING

Copyright © 1997 by Military Information Enterprises, Inc.
MIE Publishing is a subsidiary of Military Information Enterprises, Inc.

Printed in the United States of America.

MIE Publishing
PO Box 17118
Spartanburg, SC 29301
(800) 937-2133
E-mail: MIEPUB@aol.com
http://www.eden.com/~mie

Library of Congress Cataloging in Publication Data:

Ray, Don.
Checking out lawyers / by Don Ray.
        p. cm.
    Includes index,
    ISBN 1-877639-60-5
    1. Attorney and client – United States – Popular works.
2. Practice of law – United States – Popular works.
3. Lawyers – United States – Popular works. I. Title.
KF311.Z9R39   1997   96-44473
340'.02373–dc21   CIP

Disclaimer: This book is designed to provide information and is sold with the understanding that the publisher and authors are not engaged in rendering legal or other professional services.

Every effort has been made to make this book as complete and accurate as possible. There may be mistakes, either typographical or in content. Therefore, this book should be used as a general guide.

The authors or MIE Publishing shall have neither liability nor responsibility to any person regarding any loss or damage caused or alleged to be caused directly or indirectly by the information contained in this book.

This book is intended to help you, the reader, make a more informed decision about choosing a lawyer. It is not a substitute for your independent judgement, which you can and should exercise after using this book and interviewing your potential attorney.

Because of the controversial nature of this subject matter, we have edited out all references to real people and situations to illustrate our points. Therefore, any relationship between any individual and situation in this book and any real person or situation is purely coincidental.

To my loving mother, Doris Quinn,
for believing in me the way only a mother can.

Acknowledgments

There were a lot of people who pitched in and offered their valuable time, advice, referrals or just plain moral support that enabled me to complete this book.

Two very special people volunteered dozens of hours on the Internet. Patricia Kaehler in Ohio and Linda Rael in the state of Washington sent out scores of electronic questionnaires to lawyers, judges, paralegals, legal secretaries and their clients so that we could accurately represent the feelings and opinions of people involved in the field of law. Thanks to both of you. Michele Harvey used the old-fashioned telephone to gather the same type of information. Thanks, Michele.

I must also thank Drew Sullivan, Alan Schlein, Cory de Vera, Rosemary Armao, Tim Redmond, Dawn Hobbes, Bruce Shapior, Jon Duffey, Tracy Barnett, Don Holland and all the other members of Investigative Reporters and Editors, Inc. who offered materials and referrals. And thanks also to Rebecca Daugherty of the Reporter's Committee for Freedom of the Press.

Retired Judge Harry Shafer, Ed Consigilio, Mark Pollack, Dan Schmidt, J.D. Lord, Ken Olson, Chuck Campbell, and Maureen Gerwig set aside valuable time to give me detailed information. Chuck Campbell and Russell Revlin put me in touch with valuable contacts.

Among the many legal professionals I want to thank are Kevin E. Balfe, Elizabeth A. Barranco, Sam Hochberg, Mark E. Kauffelt, Stephanie A. McManus, Kim Newbrough, Dick Thory and Grace Wagner.

And there were those who provided other kinds of special help—Cindi Ishigaki and her family, Nancy Revlin, David Ritchie, Tom Newmark, Victor Cook, Carolyn Alvarado, Julie

Seltzer, Stuart Hunter, George Vejar, Gene Giddings, David Stiebel, Ralph E. Barrett, Dr. John McDevitt, Pat Murkland, Melanie Paek, Dianne and Erin Heath, Gladis Howard, Elmer and Gabriela Romero, Eric Edwardson, Dave Holland, Nancy and Jack Holland, Karl Voss, Bob and Gail Ginger, Susan Wilcox, Sossy Kassajikian, Artineh Haven, Russ Koogler, Elsa Cordero, Ernest Garcia, Joe and Jason Veraldi, Dale Martin, Neal Velgos, Joanne Van Hook and my dear friend Carlos Ponce, who died before he could reach his twentieth birthday.

A special thanks to the people responsible for me writing this book and for the quality of the final product. This list includes Dick Bielen, who recommended me as the author; Debbie Knox and Dick Johnson, the publishers who took a chance on me; Tom Ninkovich, who did all the great editing; and Celia Rocks, the world's greatest promoter.

And thanks to all whose names I may have overlooked.

How to Use This Book

If you just bought this book, let me be the first to thank you. If you're considering buying it, you won't need to read very far to see that this book could be the cat's meow. If you're just looking to glean some quick information, you can't possibly memorize all the important stuff here unless you're the Rain Man or something. And you'd better read this section quickly because that store clerk over there has been watching you since you came in.

If you're fixing to steal it, be careful. The police just might arrest you, and they'll probably take this book as evidence. Then when your trial comes up, you'll be floundering without the one book that might have saved your backside. And besides, if you *are* stealing this book, what the heck are you doing reading it in the bookstore? Is this your first caper?

At the very least, the information in this book can help you do some perfunctory things everyone ought to do before they get too involved with any attorney. It'll help you decide if you even need an attorney. You'll discover some interesting alternatives. That's right there in Chapter One ("Do You Really Need a Lawyer?"). Be sure to read that part first.

You can skip Chapter Two ("Finding the Right Attorney") if you already know which lawyer you want to check out. If you're trying to choose an attorney, check some powerful tips that may just help you weed out the strays and losers.

Chapter Three ("The State Bar") is a must-read for everyone. That's because every attorney has to be a member of his state bar association. Here is where you'll find the quickest way to check out an attorney through the state bar, as well as the right questions to ask.

You may want to know what kind of student that attorney was. Then take a drive through Chapter Four ("Law Schools"). Do you really want an attorney who was still throwing spit wads six years after high school?

Now, the shoppers who didn't read this far never got to find out that the back of this book is a gold mine of information you can use to check out anyone. It's true. Chapter Five ("Using Public Records") explains how much incredible information is available to the public in government offices. Specifically, you'll learn about records and things at city or town hall, at the various courts, at the state level, and finally at the federal level.

By then, you'll be treading water in information you've collected. Then the last chapter ("How to Use the Information") tells you what to do with all this information and how to be discreet about it.

The three appendices will put you on the right track towards useful references such as addresses, phone numbers, e-mail addresses and URLs. Appendix A covers Internet and Web sites. Appendix B gives all kinds of information at the state level. And Appendix C goes into detail about federal resources.

All in all, you'll be on information overload if you take all the tips in this book. And if you have even the most primitive sense of humor, you're sure to chuckle along the way. I know I did writing it.

Oh, and to the book thief: that woman with the book bag has been videotaping you. You better bail out and buy this book. You know you're hooked—you've read this far.

Table of Contents

Chapter One

☑ *Do You Really Need a Lawyer?*

A book on how to check out your lawyer? I could think of a hundred things I'd rather be doing than writing this stuff down. And I'm sure there's stuff you'd rather be doing than reading it. Then why are we both doing this? Aren't all those high-priced attorneys out there supposed to be protecting us and defending us and generally looking after us? Then why do we have to be checking them out? We don't go to this trouble to check out the local deputy sheriff or the paramedics.

The sad truth is that, lately, too many of those rascal lawyers haven't been minding the store very well. Maybe it's because they don't have some desk sergeant or battalion commander watching over them all day long. Whatever the reason, there are a few renegades who are either sleeping on the job or staying up nights conjuring up ways to pick our pockets. Some of them are outright fleecing us. I think you'd agree it's high time we put a stop to it. Some folks out there are madder than a half-swatted hornet.

Trouble is, those bad-apple attorneys—the ones causing all the trouble—well, they're a slippery bunch. Before you realize you're dealing with a bad one, your wallet's gone and he's just grinning at you. He took your money and there's not too much you can do about it once it's done.

You see, lawyers are in a unique sort of position. They're in a kind of brotherhood. In many ways they speak their own secret language and dress in their own uniforms and generally hang out together. There's really no one scrutinizing them except other lawyers. They seem to show great respect to judges, but judges are nothing more than lawyers in black robes who, at least once, had good political connections. The lawyers and the judges base everything they do on laws—laws generally written by lawyers. It's kind of incestuous, isn't it? Go sit in a courtroom some morning and watch two attorneys battle each other as if they were lifelong rivals—the Hatfields and McCoys. Then step over to the nearby coffee shop at lunch and see who's sitting together, carrying on about their golf or tennis match this weekend.

It would be a delight if we didn't have to even associate with attorneys. No hard feelings—just let them live their lives and we'd live ours. Peaceful coexistence. But just when you think everything's going fine, someone comes along and sues you in court, or some crooked soul cheats you out of something, or even worse, you find yourself arrested and in jail for some foolish thing, and all of a sudden you need a lawyer. And you pray that yours isn't one of those scoundrels.

You're going to want to keep this little book handy in case of emergencies because it's going to help you make pretty darn certain the lawyer you end up with is one of the good, honest, hard-working kind.

Now let me get this straight right away. I'm not a guy who just categorically despises attorneys. Actually, some of my best friends are attorneys. I even let them come over to the house and play with my dog and all. Don't think that just because I'm going to show you a zillion ways a crooked or lazy attorney could do you in that I'm an attorney basher or anything. In fact, if you're a lawyer reading this book, I'm sure you're one of the good ones who make up the vast majority of legal professionals. This book is probably just a refresher course for you on how not to screw up.

Oh, and if you're a woman attorney or one of those politically correct folks who thinks the word "she" ought to get equal time with "he" and all that stuff, just forget it here. Chill out. Everyone's a "he" in this book because it makes it a lot easier to read (and to write, for that matter). I can hear your argument already—"Hey, Don Ray. Why don't you just use 'she' throughout the whole book? Huh?" Well you should have figured that out by now. If I did that, I'd have every woman in the country coming after me for implying that only women lawyers are crooked, and I'm sure that's not the case.

*   *   *   *

Okay, now that we've decided that the book is useful and we've agreed on its gender and all, let's roll up our sleeves and get to work. I'm going to show you a heckuva lot of ways to learn all kinds of things about that attorney of yours.

But first, you've got to ask yourself a very important question, "Do I really need a lawyer? Isn't there some way I can get by without one?" In a lot of circumstances the answer is "You betcha!" In fact, there are some areas where I think you're better off without an attorney.

Remember, attorneys need money to buy their BMWs and Rolex watches and designer strollers for their kids. Many of them get that money from clients who are somehow involved in a dispute of some sort. It could be a dispute with the government over a law some policeman thinks you broke, or a dispute between two entities—such as you and a business, you and another person or even you and your spouse.

If you've been arrested, don't even consider not using an attorney. But if you're involved in a dispute with another person or with a business, you may actually lose more money winning with an attorney than losing without one. And if you're involved in a divorce and you bring in an attorney, everyone's apt to lose—that is, everyone except the attorneys. Understand one very important fact of life: As long as you keep on fighting, the lawyers keep on making money. Why would they want to see the battle end? That's why I say to you that maybe you should be looking at another way of resolving the dispute. In fact, are you sure you really have a full-fledged dispute on your hands?

A good friend of mine, Dr. David Stiebel, makes a good living helping folks resolve disputes. He may be hired by a group of neighbors who don't want that new prison built nearby (such folks are called NIMBYs—an acronym for Not In My Back Yard). Or he may be getting paid by the city government which hopes to cash in on all the new jobs a prison might bring in. One of the first things Dr. David does is try to figure out if they've got a real, live dispute on their hands or just a problem understanding each other—a communications problem.

For instance, the NIMBYs may just outright assume there

are going to be murderers and rapists living within a stone's throw of their kids' playgrounds. Dr. David will get both sides talking and find out that the prison will house only white collar criminals. All of a sudden the NIMBYs don't object anymore.

"If simple clarification results in the problem going away," says Dr. David, "then there never was a dispute in the first place. It was just a communication problem." If either side had dragged in a lawyer, it might very well have started some kind of chain reaction. "Heck," one side would say, "if *they've* got a dang lawyer, well we ought to have ourselves one too." Pretty soon both sides are scratching each others' eyes out.

And even if better communications doesn't make the problem go away, Dr. David is real good at helping one side figure out what would make the other side want to agree on stuff. That can lead to a painless and inexpensive resolution. But if those attorneys get in there, often times battle lines are drawn and neither side is willing to show its cards—much less back down or compromise.

What makes using a *dispute resolution specialist* such as Dr. David so wonderful is that either side can hire him. People, companies, associations and government agencies have saved millions of dollars by hiring Dr. David. He's quite famous, you know. He's my buddy.

In the legal world they call this Alternative Dispute Resolution or A.D.R. Another A.D.R. method is for both sides to agree to a *mediator*. A mediator is similar to Dr. David except both parties agree up front to let a mediator, a neutral third party, get involved. The mediator will listen to the rantings and ravings of both sides, read all the supporting documents or whatever, and then decide what he thinks is fair. Either side can tell him to go pound sand—his suggestions are not at all binding.

But hopefully, the mediator can get both parties to stop acting like sniveling two-year-olds and get them to agree on something—anything.

But many times, one of the two arguing parties will fold his arms, shake his head and say, "Not on your life," to the non-binding suggestions of the mediator. So for those I-don't-have-to-do-what-you-say donkeys there's yet another way of not giving a pair of lawyers the whole piggy bank. They can agree to turn over their guns and ammo to an *arbitrator.* This fella steps into the picture only when both of the pouting parties promise they'll put their hankies away and do whatever the arbitrator thinks is fair. No more pouting. No appeals. Tough luck.

Another way to keep things from getting out of hand is to agree to an *early neutral evaluation.* Both sides agree to hire a neutral evaluator. His job is to look over everything both sides bring to the table and see if he can't find a way to settle things. One nice thing about his job is that he doesn't have to watch the two squabble in person. Each side comes in, either with or without an attorney, and tells its version of things. If either side wants to make an offer, the evaluator will present it to the other side. That way the other side is likely to be less suspicious and less likely throw a temper tantrum. And even if the two sides dig in their heels and refuse to settle, the neutral evaluator can at least help both of them see areas where they tend to agree. He can assess the strengths and weaknesses of each side's case and maybe even get both parties to hand over things for free before their attorneys charge a small fortune to have a judge order it.

A second cousin to an early neutral evaluation is a *voluntary settlement conference.* In this case a neutral settlement officer does his best to convince both sides to compromise. A lot of times this expert will paint a pretty dreary picture of what's going to happen if they take this ugly dispute to court. If he does his job well, the two sides will see the light, shake hands and maybe go out for a beer afterward.

A *summary jury trial* may just be the magic potion some folks need. Get this: The two sides actually go out and hire themselves a "judge"—some disinterested third party—and then hire at least six people to be the jury. The "judge" oversees short presentations by both sides and lets the jury decide the outcome. The two parties can either agree to accept what the jury says or use the "verdict" to help them come to some settlement agreement.

Any of these little tricks could save you a bundle. Now don't you start feeling sorry for the poor lawyers. I promise you they won't starve. Let them dip into someone else's well. You can check with your local court clerk for lists of alternative methods of resolving disputes. Or, just check your local yellow pages under Arbitrators or Mediation Services.

There's also hope for you hollering husbands and wives out there who swear you'd rather pour hot grease down a grizzly's back than stay married—at least to your current spouse. Can any of you relate? You're probably not going to do back flips when you first read this, but hang on—there's some pretty good logic at work here. Suppose, just suppose, the two of you simply agreed to agree one time, and agree on just one thing—that you both care about your kids more than you care about some blood-sucking lawyer.

Does it sound crazy? Stay tuned, pal. Here's the logic: If either one of you goes bawling to an attorney, then the other is sure to feel as vulnerable as a trout in a bucket. Of course, that's going to send him or her running to hire an opposing lawyer. The attorney trap now slams shut. From here on in, anything one attorney files in court will automatically result in a filing by the other side. With each filing comes another bill for services and, sure enough, another filing by the side that filed the first filing. This filing stuff can go on and on for years—that is, if the lawyers have their way. If you were to add up all the money the typical embattled couple hands over to the attorneys, you'd realize it was enough to send a kid or two to college.

Get the idea? It's a matter of creative comparing. Who are the people both you and your spouse love more than anyone? It's the kids, right? Okay, stay with me on this one. And you'd both agree that your kids are more important to you than a pair of lawyers, right? Okay, then would the two of you agree that you would rather see the $5,000 to $50,000 go to a college fund for the kids, and administered by some neutral third party who won't let either of you get your destructive hands on the money? You would agree to that, wouldn't you? I'll bet even that sorry-looking spouse of yours would have to go along with such a brilliant plan. Don't try approaching your not-so-better half face-to-face on this one. Unless you're really communicating well, you might want to send a note. And it doesn't even have to be a nice note. Here's a sample you can use:

Dear Jerkface:

You stink. Hate your guts. Would love to see you buried, neck-deep in a colony of fire ants. The only good thing about you is that you're the parent of my children. I know that you care about them—after all, the part I contributed to them makes them great children. Who couldn't love them?

Listen carefully, Fatso. Without realizing it, we've just agreed on one thing. We both care about our kids. Do you care more about the kids than you do about that moron attorney of yours? Bet you do.

Okay, here's a plan that even someone as stupid as you can com-

prehend (even without color-coding and pictures): Let's give our attorneys the boot and divert the money we would have wasted on them into a trust account that can be used only for the kids' college education.

One of us can write up a fair agreement and the other can select the person who'll act as trustee. I know you're an idiot, but I don't think you're such a lowlife that you'd steal money from your own kids.

What do you think, Peanutbrain?

Your loving spouse,

Think what you may, the chances are real good that this'll work. And, if you're feeling the least bit generous or compassionate, you can soften it a bit—maybe change Peanutbrain to Walnutbrain.

Now, you may be saying, "Don Ray, you're dumber than a box of hair. It'll never work." I know some folks in the Midwest who were perfect candidates for my brilliant plan. Dick and Jane were going through one of the fiercest divorces I've ever seen. Did you ever try locking up a bobcat and a pitbull in a phone booth? Well, that would be a friendly game of checkers compared to the fighting these two were doing. They were arrested so many times during their battles that the local police considered opening up a sub-station in their garage. Their attorneys were like two mosquitoes in a nudist colony. One would file a motion and then send a bill. The other would counter and send a bill. Motion, bill, counter, bill, counter-motion, bill, counter-counter-motion, bill, and so on. The fighting got so fierce the two of them were out borrowing money so they could shovel it to the attorneys.

No, I wasn't able to convince Dick and Jane to back down.

It's like trying to separate two fighting dogs without a hose. But Dick and Jane's neighbors, Ken and Barbie (did you figure out yet I've changed the names?) had also decided to split up and they gravitated to the same two lawyers who were sucking Jane and Dick dry. I had a ·chance to sit down with Ken as he was writing out one of the early checks to his attorney. "Couldn't that money be going to your kid's education instead of to some slimy lawyer?" I asked him.

His response was typical—sure, he'd go for it in a split second, but he was sure Barbie wouldn't. They all say that. But after I badgered him awhile, he caved in and wrote a note to her, not too much nicer than my sample up above.

"You're not going to believe it, Don Ray," he said the next day, "She agreed to give it a try!"

That was five years ago and they're still calling each other names. But the money they set aside for their daughter's education is growing as it gathers interest. Meanwhile, Jane had to sell the house she had before she married Dick. Both of their kids are fed up being the pawns in their parents' fierce chess game. In fact, Dad convinced their son that Mom is a lying thief who should be in jail. The boy has filed a civil suit against his mother seeking damages for items his mother liquidated when the couple split up. The only winners are those danged attorneys.

Another couple, Bob and Sue, divorced about five years ago and ended up with one of those joint custody situations. Sue thought things were going along just fine until one day the kids ran away from Dad's place and ended up at Mom's. They told stories of control and repression and abuse and such that made Sue believe Bob was Adolph Hitler's evil twin. Well, being the good mother she is, she told the kids to not set foot in Gestapo

Dad's place anymore. And, sure as hot fudge melts ice cream, Bob screamed "unfair!" Sue decided to do everything legally, so she brought in a hired gun—an attorney.

I think you can see what's coming. Yes, Bob hired a bigger gun—an attorney some folks likened to Ivan the Terrible—and before you could say "mediation anyone?" the fur was flying. And that's only natural. I think there's some law of nature that completely shuts down people's ears when they're involved in a full-fledged fist fight. When two people are pounding each other with anything handy, it's not a good time for you to ask, even very calmly, "Would the two of you care to negotiate?"

The interesting phenomena about couples fighting is that, once the battle starts, they both forget that there was ever even the tiniest speck of goodness in that person they married.

"What do you suppose Bob wants?" I asked Sue. I was fishing for something like, "He wants to be able to have custody of the kids." Or, "He wants to spend more time with the kids."

But her actual answer was, "He's a sick, jealous, controlling person who is determined to hurt me in any way he can." I started scratching my head as if I had lice. No matter how I pressed her, she was unwilling to admit that Bob had even one little seedling of love for the kids. And she didn't even flinch when she told me the whole battle was going to cost her at least $50,000. That's what happens. When a couple points guns at each other they forget everything that made them fall in love and get married in the first place.

A year or two after the divorce, most divorcees will probably find someone else to love—someone who doesn't see even a trace of the monster their ex saw in them. I believe this happens because they hire gasoline-toting lawyers to handle what started out to be only a spark of a dispute.

I spoke with a successful attorney who told me I was a na-
ive dreamer. She insists that an attorney is absolutely necessary
in cases where one party in the divorce has a big financial advantage over the other. And, she cautions, it may be years before the other person realizes the agreement was unfair.

If you want to get another perspective on how things work
in court, talk to a court reporter. One such court reporter,
Maureen Gerwig is her name, spent some 23 years listening to
every word spoken in open court as well as in the judges' chambers. In fact, she says the judges are sometimes as bad as or
worse than the attorneys.

"Some judges let their power go to their heads," she says.
"Not long after some judges are appointed, they start believing
they were *anointed*." After all her years in courts, she says the
courtroom is the last place some people should go.

"My advice is, stay out of court if at all possible—especially
family law courts," she says. "What makes it so bad is the in-
competence of too many judges on the bench. They're incred-
ibly inept when it comes to understanding human relations.
They're more interested in maintaining some image, but too
often, behind that image is very little substance."

She says many judges in family law court are there because
they're about to retire and want to become private judges. In
some states, people can choose to do their fighting in a private
courtroom run by a retired judge. "The problem is," Maureen
says, "they want the attorneys in the county court to bring their
business to his private court after he retires. The judge is soon
taking better care of the attorneys than he is of the divorcing
couple."

A retired judge told me the same thing. "Lately more and
more judges are asking to sit in family law courts because they

know it's an entry into being a private judge," says Harry Shafer. He spent more than 17 years as a judge in Los Angeles County. "I know of a case where one judge told everyone in his court-room he was looking for business." This is what they call an old-fashioned conflict of interest. How can a judge be fair and unbiased when he's courting attorneys to be his private clients?

Judge Shafer says that in the current system of handling divorce cases in civil court there's also a built-in conflict of in-terest between the attorney and the client.

"If the attorney settles, he's out of business," says Judge Shafer, "at least with that client. No, he's going to make sure to order lots of depositions and interrogatories and other costly things. He says he wants to 'protect the client.' Well, if he really wanted to protect the client, he'd settle. The way things are now, the people seeking the divorce are no longer the litigants—the law-yers are the litigants."

One of my lawyer friends (one of the many honest, up-standing ones) told me he's known of attorneys in similar situ-ations who have actually communicated with each other through some middleman. They'd secretly plan out which motions they'd file—motions they were sure would keep up the momentum of their profitable divorce case. They were shar-ing the care and feeding of their goose that laid golden eggs.

I sat down and chatted with several veteran (and honest) judges and they unanimously agreed that family law matters such as divorces and custody fights should be yanked out of civil court. No attorneys ought to be involved, they agreed. They preferred a system where the divorcing couple lays out every-thing in front of a family counselor, an accountant, and a re-tired judge. No lawyers. This panel would decide what's best for the sanity of the kids, what's fair financially, and what's legal. One judge suggested the panel split everything as evenly as possible and then let the couple decide which person gets which half of the pie. The couple would have to somehow agree or risk losing some or all of what the panel offered.

This, the judges agreed, would nip in the bud the temptation some lawyers would have to milk their clients out of their life savings.

There are not nearly enough non-adversarial marriage dissolution services around. I was able to locate one in Southern California that is remarkably similar to the judge/counselor/accountant concept I mentioned earlier. The people at the Olive Branch Counseling Centers in Rancho Cucamonga and Riverside operate their mediation service on the theory that it's the children who often come out of a divorce licking the most wounds.

"The kids become the emotional pawns when the parents go through traditional litigation," says its director, Ken Olson, a licensed marriage and family counselor who's also a trained mediator. "They end up becoming the messengers or victims of their parents' emotional baggage. The parents try holding up visitations or child support as hostages to punish each other." When couples come to the nonprofit center, they work with both a therapist and an attorney who help them keep their anger and fighting in check while they work out a fair settlement agreement. And while Olive Branch doesn't bring in a money advisor, the counselors often encourage the couple to talk to an accountant or tax specialist who may just help them turn cash conflicts into creative compromises. Of course, this only happens after the counselors have thoroughly removed the claws from the couples' paws.

"A divorce done through attorneys never allows for emotional closure the way a funeral does," says Olson. "When some-one dies, the wake, funeral and burial allow family members a chance to say 'goodbye' and then move on. Our mediation is similar to a funeral in that it gives couples the chance to say 'goodbye' to the dreams they once had of a happy marriage and to the emotions that come up during the split-up." In fact, they even break out a bottle of the bubbly, clink their glasses and wish each other the best.

"Once the paperwork is done," says Olson, "there is closure." And, he says, the cost of their mediation can easily be a mere fraction of what they would pay a pair of hired-gun attorneys.

Remember, it's a real temptation to let the fight continue. Granted, I'm sure a lot of attorneys out there would never try to exploit their clients and milk the proverbial cash cow. But when the feathers are a flyin,' the meter's a runnin.' And even an honest attorney can easily sit back and just let the fists fly. I can imagine one of those few bad attorneys going home after a long day in divorce court. "Hi, Honey, I'm home. What a day I've had. You wouldn't believe how two grown-ups can go at each other. I'm tuckered out after all that fighting. By the way, we may have enough now for that vacation home in the south of France and a pair of new Mercedes for Missy and Sharky Junior."

Just like ants at a picnic, we're never going to be without attorneys. At least attorneys are sometimes useful. But there *are* folks out there willing to help you take care of your legal prob-lems without a lawyer. Check out the fine people at Nolo Press in Berkeley, California. The company's sole purpose of being is to help people handle legal situations without using attorneys. Their store is chock full of their own and other people's legal self-help books. You can phone them at (800) 728-3555 or e-mail them at cs@Nolo.com. If you're on the Internet, check out their website at http://www.nolo.com. You can get a lot of answers to your legal questions right there at their site.

By the way, the Internet is a great resource for people seeking legal help. We've listed scads of online resources for you at the end of this book. But be careful. There's no guarantee that anything you pick up out there in cyberspace isn't tainted or stolen or just plain untrue. One of the first things you should download off the Nolo Press website is their piece titled "Online Legal Advice: Let the Browser Beware." It gives good advice about considering the source, checking to be sure the information is up-to-date, making sure the stuff you're getting online is legal in your state, getting a reference, being sure you understand everything about the legal forms you can download, and how to go to the right places for the right kind of help. The Nolo Press website also has the best collection of lawyer jokes I've run across.

Joke about lawyers if you like, but you'll probably have to hire one if you can't snuff out that dispute before it makes it to the courthouse. However, before you sign on the dotted line with any attorney, you'd better check him out.

Chapter Two

☑ *Finding the Right Attorney*

If you have already chosen an attorney, you can probably just skip this chapter. This is for the folks who need some help on how to select the right attorney out of the crowd. Or, if you've already checked out your existing attorney and decided to give him the boot, this chapter will help you do a better job of selecting the next one.

Unfortunately, there's no easy way of finding an attorney who's right for you. After all, we need different kinds of attorneys for different needs, different problems. It's very much akin to finding the right person to solve a medical problem. You wouldn't go to a podiatrist to yank a tooth or to an optometrist to clear up that rash you picked up last week. You wouldn't fly to the Mayo Clinic for a flu shot, nor would you let your kind, old, family doctor do intricate brain surgery on you. It's easy to get referrals in the world of medicine, but a whole lot tougher when it comes to finding the right lawyer.

There are a lot of on-ramps to finding the right lawyer, and experts can't seem to agree which is best. I polled a lot of folks in a lot of areas of the law and was able to whittle down all their great advice to a sort of top-ten list. Each one has its advantages and disadvantages. You'll have to consider the value of each one based on your own needs, resources, degree of laziness and gut feeling. By the way, these aren't in any particular order.

1. Advertisements. This is just about the easiest way to learn the names of attorneys serving your area. Just stay home from work one day and watch local television. By watching daytime commercials you'll think every single person watching TV is either sick as a dog, a moron in need of career training, an irregular or incontinent octogenarian or a victim of an accident in need of a personal-injury lawyer. Understand that if you first heard an attorney's name in a TV or radio ad, you're only getting the information he wants you to have. He's probably a specialist, has a lot of attorneys working for him, and must generate a lot of business to keep paying for the expensive ads. If you've been seeing or hearing the ads for the past ten years, at least you know he's been around awhile. Does that make him a good attorney? Not necessarily. Might be he's a personal-injury lawyer who takes in hundreds of cases a month on a contingency basis—that is, the client doesn't have to put up any money. The attorney takes a piece (usually a pretty good piece: 30-40%) of any settlement money or judgement money. In the course of the month, he settles enough of the easy ones to afford all those TV and radio spots.

Yellow page ads are a different story. You're going to see a variety of ads by all kinds of lawyers. And attorneys' ads don't just speak to you, THEY SHOUT! Before you've had time to find the beginning of the attorneys' section, you'll wish they made earplugs for your eyes.

"Criminal Defense!" "Personal Injury!" "Bankruptcy?" "Accidents: No Recovery, No Fee!" "Injured?" "Free Consultation!" "Sexual Harassment or Discrimination?" "Divorce!" Of course, there's one very large ad that's much more subtle. It shows an attractive, conservative, confident couple with pleasant smiles on their faces. No bold type. No shouting. In fact, the half-page ad is surrounded by a pleasant green border—mild compared to the glaring reds of other ads. It only takes a few seconds, though, to realize the border is that of a larger-than-life dollar bill. Honestly, I never felt so solicited since 1968 when I walked with other young soldiers past the bars and clubs along Kadena Gate Two Street in Okinawa. It was the same concept—coming from every direction. "Hey, G.I.! Stateside show!" "No, G.I., over here! Show start in five minutes!" "Come in here! Free drinks!" "Pretty girls!" "Snake dancer!"

I also remember the more mild-mannered solicitor whose style was very much akin to the attorney couple in the dollar bill ad. He was an Asian, dressed neatly, and not shouting like the others along the block. Instead, when we approached he spoke in a deep voice without the slightest accent. "Good evening, gentlemen. Hope you're enjoying yourselves tonight. Say, you might consider stepping into our club here. We have a wonderful show starting in just a few, short minutes. Come in. Have a free drink and enjoy our beautiful girls." It was just too weird. We passed on it. There was certainly no shortage of places to unload our money.

And there's no shortage of attorneys, either. You won't have any trouble finding an attorney who handles cases similar to yours. Trouble is, like those TV ads, nothing guarantees these folks are any better than the modest ones who don't buy big ads. If you're lucky, your yellow pages will have a section where they break down the attorneys by specialty. In that part, you won't have to listen to their loud, screaming ads.

One attorney told me he looks at the ads to see what the lawyer or firm wants to convey about their operation. "Their ad might make you think they occupy two entire floors of a high-rise. So be leery when you show up and find them renting the back of a shoe store." Or as a Texan attorney put it, "You wanna be careful. They may be all hat and no cattle."

If you want to search no further, the ads may be your cup of tea. But don't come crying to me when he turns out to be nothing more than a money vacuum.

2. Referrals from friends. Absolutely. If there's someone in your family or at work or in your circle of friends who's been happy with a particular attorney, it can't hurt to check him out. You kill a couple of birds with that stone. First, you're likely to find someone in your area who, most likely, uses the same court you may be using. Second, you can be assured the attorney was able to please at least one client. That's a step above using just the yellow pages. It's certainly worth giving this guy a call and seeing if you like what he has to say. The other advantage of talking to him is that, while he may not be the lawyer you ultimately grab onto, he may very well know an attorney who's just right for you.

But just because someone else liked him doesn't mean he can handle your particular case any better than one of those yellow page guys. Your friend may have used him for a property dispute while you need someone to help you with family law stuff. But call him anyway. Most attorneys know pretty well who's good in town and who's bad. The referral becomes a good starting point. You might ask him to give you the names of four or five attorneys he thinks could handle your problem. The fact that you're a friend or relative of one of his happy clients will greatly enhance your chances of getting a well-thought-out response.

One lawyer suggests being cautious about referrals from satisfied clients. "The satisfied clients may have had a simple, high-dollar case that any schmuck attorney could do, and the client might not know that."

There's no harm in asking around. I doubt you'd need to ask more than about five people before someone gave you a suggestion about an attorney they've been happy with or a referral to one of their friends who's had good luck with an attorney. Once you're talking to an attorney somebody trusts, you're at least in a better position to find out who he would use if he were in your situation. Read on.

3. Lawyer referrals. This method, by far, was the most popular method among the dozens of attorneys I talked with across the U.S.—and it makes sense. An attorney is more likely to know more attorneys and have an idea about the reputation of any given attorney. The first step is to approach an attorney—any attorney with a good reputation. It could be one who handled a case of yours once, a friend's attorney, an attorney you read favorable things about in the newspaper, or even an attorney you know who whopped someone's backside in court. If all else fails, you could simply grab the yellow pages and start calling lawyers in your area at random. If you do it this way, however, be sure to talk with at least five or six. After a few calls you'll start hearing the same names over and over again. Now you're on the right track.

When you get the lawyer on the phone, politely tell him you're in the market for an attorney to solve a particular problem. For example, "I'm looking for an attorney here in Jackson County to help me draw up a family trust. Could you recommend three or four reputable attorneys who could handle this?" There's a chance the attorney will offer his services. That's fine and dandy. Put him on your list of potential attorneys and move on. More likely, though, he's going to give you a few names. If not, he may send you to one attorney he knows who would be more likely to know attorneys with that specialty.

I've had good luck with asking the question, "If you needed an attorney to draw up a family trust (or whatever task you need done), who would you use?" Several attorneys told me they'd be happy to call around to lawyers they knew well and ask them for referrals.

"In some fields of law," says one attorney, "there is even a financial incentive for your local attorney to find someone good. It's called fee-splitting. In many jurisdictions and for most types of law, it's legitimate so long as you receive a document in writing that says that the client is not being charged any greater fee than customary for the case." In other words, your local attorney might get a "finder's fee" payable out of the attorney fees collected by the active attorney. This is more common in personal injury and malpractice claims, and is usually to the benefit of the client.

A friend of mine in the Midwest won more than three million dollars in a discrimination suit against a county government that had let him go. I asked him how he picked his lawyer. Turns out he got a referral from another attorney—but his method and motive were unlike anything I'd ever seen. I still have to laugh when I think about it.

"I called a lawyer friend and asked him for the names of three attorneys who specialized in wrongful termination cases. I called the first one and made an appointment for a one-hour consultation. I was willing to pay for this because I knew exactly what I wanted.

"It was clear from the minute I walked in that this was not the attorney for me. He was too nice. Too polite. He looked too caring. I wasted no time. I asked him, 'Who is the one attorney you dread most going up against in court? Who do you hate the most? Who makes you shudder when you think about opposing him?' He didn't even pause to think about it—he gave me the name followed by, 'that son of a bitch!' I knew I had found the right attorney for this case.

"I made an appointment and went to meet with this hated attorney. I'll never forget it. I walked in and there was this creature sitting at his desk. He was sleazy. He was unkempt. He had such bad breath you'd think he just ate four onion sandwiches. I remember the light shining from the window behind him. It silhouetted these huge hairs growing out of his ears. I swear I wanted to lean over and yank them out—or at least say something about them.

"Then I looked into those eyes of his. He looked through me. He looked like he had the key to your back closet and knew where you kept all your secrets hidden. He represented everything you would not want going up against you. One look at him and I knew he was the enemy and I was glad he was on my side."

4. The local bar association. Most counties or large metropolitan areas have a local bar association that is happy to refer you to a lawyer. The lawyer they refer you to will almost always be one of their members. And it's not in their interest to say anything nasty about their members. In fact, they may not even be allowed to recommend a "best" attorney. Don't want to anger those other members.

Mark Pollack, one of the most reputable attorneys I've ever encountered, says checking with the local bar can, at times, be a good thing. "Find out if they are a member. Membership alone is significant. Oftentimes those seat-of-the pants practitioners who will rob Peter to pay Paul won't pay their local bar dues." Mark says he doesn't attend the meetings of the local bar association. He's a member because his local bar puts on Mandatory Continuing Legal Education (M.C.L.E.) classes. These are short courses required by most states to keep attorneys abreast of things in the legal field.

"I belong so that I can get the M.C.L.E. hours. The local bar puts on programs for the cost of lunch and membership. I'd be suspicious of a lawyer who wouldn't belong just for the classes."

5. National expert referral. This is my own trick, but it'll work well for you, too. As a journalist, I often need to find an expert quickly because of some pending deadline. A lot of times I don't know diddly about a particular subject and I need to find someone to educate me quickly. But I need someone I can trust really knows the subject and has no reason to lie to me. Here's what I do. I find someone locally who knows about the overall subject—a lot of times I go through a local university to get plugged into the right person. Then I ask the local guy who the best in the entire nation is—or at least what school is known to be the best.

When I zero in on the expert-of-all-experts, I call him and ask him to point me to the person he thinks is best in my area. When I chat with the local referral, I usually get someone who will clue me in about the situation in his field and someone who will, in his own way, let me know if the person I'm investigating is a scoundrel or a fake.

You can do the very same thing. Find an expert in any city, call him and ask him to refer you to an attorney in your area that he knows is good in his field. By going to the expert-of-all-experts, you're almost guaranteed to reel in the best one in your neck of the woods. What also happens is that the local expert you wind up with will be tickled that the referral came from someone he really admires and respects. Out of fear of word getting back to the big expert, your local attorney will probably treat you even better than if you'd called him cold.

6. Attorney directories. If you really want to do it right, you're going to have to get off your duff and run down to the nearest law library and crack open the *Martindale-Hubbard Law Directory.* You may also find it in larger public libraries. The directory lists attorneys by state and city. It'll give you information about attorneys' backgrounds, specialties, things they've gotten involved with in the bar association and more. The part you're going to be most interested in is how it rates the attorney based on his legal skills, ethics and professionalism. Most lawyers show up in the directory, so you should have no trouble picking out a few who look good to you. If you can't make it to a law library, call a reference librarian at the biggest public library in your area. The reference librarian will tell you what similar books are available at that library and maybe even at other nearby libraries.

7. Presiding judge. Since you've bothered to go look in the law library, you might as well drive over to the courthouse. It's probably only a stone's throw from the library. Read the directory to find out the name of the presiding judge. Then head straight to his courtroom.

Now, there are a few things you need to know before you go into any courtroom—especially if you wish to talk to the judge. When you walk in, the court will likely be in session. Don't let that ruffle your feathers. Just walk in quietly and immediately sit down in the very first seat you see. It's usually in the back row. Sit there until the slight interruption caused by your entry simmers down and everyone is back focused on what's going on among the judge, the lawyers, and the witnesses. Your next job is to look around for the bailiff. He's going to have a little table or desk near the gate that separates the court officers from the spectators.

Next move? Look for a seat in the front row that's very close to the bailiff's desk. Ever so quietly, walk directly to that seat and park there. I promise you the bailiff will know you're wanting to talk to him. He'll ask if you need something. You let him know you'd like to talk to the judge about a personal matter. He may try to screen you out, but if you're polite and you don't back down, he'll probably pick up the phone and call the clerk who's sitting at the desk nearest the bench. They'll whisper to each other for a while and eventually he'll tell you to sit still until the next recess.

When the judge declares a recess, the clerk will allow him to go to his chambers. Then she'll contact him and tell him some citizen wants to chat about some personal matter. Eventually, the clerk or bailiff will invite you to the judge's chamber. That's when you politely tell him you're looking for a really good attorney. He'll probably tell you he has to be impartial. That's when you whip out your list of attorney prospects and let him look it over.

Now don't expect him to boldly commit himself. Here's where you have to look for subtle messages. Maybe a frown, a slight shake of the head or an only slightly audible grumble. You should be able to figure out either the ones he thinks are bad or those he likes.

"Keep in mind that while judges seek to be independent," writes attorney Richard Alexander on his incredible Internet website (http://www.seamless.com), "they are also, in many states, elected. To be re-elected requires popular support of the bar and the electorate. Do not be surprised if the local presiding judge declines to comment, but don't be afraid to ask. Experienced trial lawyers have used this technique from time to time. Keep in mind that you may learn more by what a judge does not say than by what he says. As long as you're cordial, explain that you have a problem, and ask for guidance, there are very few judges who will turn down your request."

8. Court personnel. Heck, you're already down at the courthouse. Most attorneys agree that court clerks, bailiffs and court reporters have a keen insight into who's good and who's not. This won't always be the easiest thing to pull off, but if you can strike up a conversation and not appear to be too strange, you might just get one of them to sing. They know who the bulldogs are, who the slobs are, and who the lazy ones are. Try going to the courthouse cafeteria and look for either a uniformed bailiff or the face of a clerk or reporter you saw in court. Park yourself at their table and get them talking about themselves. People love to talk about themselves. "What an interesting job you have," you might say. After they've chatted a bit about themselves, try something such as "I'll bet you've seen it all in your courtroom." Maybe they'll tell a few war stories. Then you can ask them who they think is the best lawyer. I'll bet you lunch they help you out.

9. Paralegals and legal secretaries. A lot of paralegals and legal secretaries work independently and, therefore, have poked around in more than a few law firms. They also talk with others in their profession. They socialize and they gossip. Again, if you've come up with a list of possible attorneys, a paralegal or legal secretary may tell you which of those on your list you should embrace and which ones you should run from.

10. The Internet. The day is coming when most every transaction you engage in is going to, somewhere along the line, be done on the Internet. If you've surfed the net, you probably already know how absolutely awesome this tool is. There isn't anything that doesn't have some website or some chat group or some news list. You can use any of the search engines as a start (these are services that jump off your screen when you're online and offer to help you find anything). Just type the word "attorney" and tell the thing to fetch. You'll soon find one site that sends you to another and another. These connections are called *links*. Eventually, you'll end up finding a listing of all the attorneys in your state or city or region. Some will be just part of long lists. Others will have their own websites (a website is like a living yellow page ad).

Remember, though, that the same precautions you have with ads in the yellow pages apply to the Internet. See Appendix A for a whole bundle of Internet resources.

Any one of the above techniques should help you find a good candidate to be your lawyer. Now you need to really check him out.

Read on.

Chapter Three

☑ *The State Bar*

By now you should already have a lawyer you want to check out or investigate. If you do nothing else to ensure he's fit to practice, you must check him out with the state bar. It's going to be the easiest phone call you ever made. And while it's certainly not going to tell you everything about an attorney, if there's something there, you definitely want to know.

The state bar is the organization that, in essence, licenses attorneys to practice law. It's a lot like the medical board, the contractors' licensing board, the bureau of automotive repair and others. It's supposed to make sure everyone participating in the field has minimum training, passes an examination to show proficiency, and is continuing their education by taking M.C.L.E. (Mandatory Continuing Legal Education) courses. And, as with other licensing agencies, the state bar listens to complaints from concerned citizens, investigates allegations of wrongdoing and takes disciplinary action, if necessary.

The main difference between a state bar and most other licensing agencies is that, usually, the state bar is not a government agency—at best, it's a quasi-government agency. Stands to reason. If lawyers make the laws and lawyers make the rules, you can bet they're going to make the rules that govern themselves. They wouldn't want to put attorney oversight in the hands of nonlawyers. God forbid. So a bunch of lawyers look after each other and they call it a bar association.

Contrary to what would seem downright logical to assume, it has nothing to do with the kind of bars we visit after work. The entire group of attorneys is called the bar because they are all privileged enough to set foot in that part of the courtroom where the general public can't go. As you'll recall from watching Perry Mason, a big old wooden bar keeps the public out of the area where the legal work takes place. Attorneys are allowed inside the bar. It's a lot like those signs at car dealerships that say you can't go into the garage and watch what the mechanic is doing to your car.

Anyway, the association of people allowed to cross that bar is called the bar association. This association also devises a test to make sure lawyers remember what they studied and know how to navigate within the courtroom and among all the laws their pals have written. They call it the bar exam. If a lawyer doesn't pass the bar exam, he doesn't get to play. If he passes the exam, but breaks one of the rules the bar writes or does something everyone would agree lawyers shouldn't do, the bar association can take action.

But don't get too excited yet. There's always a catch. Hang around a bar association for a while and you'll learn they do a lot in secret. Some of the stuff the bar association keeps on file about lawyers is public record—meaning you or anyone else can read the material without anyone telling you to get lost.

But the truth is, a lawyer can screw up quite a bit before he's in deep enough to have his disciplinary file opened to the public. Many times, I've learned, the attorney gets his hand slapped behind closed doors but fails to follow up on promises he makes to the bar association. Only then does his file become open to where all can see it. In California, there are eight levels of discipline. Only the first one is kept from view of the common folk. The other seven are open to public inspection. What we don't know, however, is just how many lawyers are nailed at the first level. Here's what can happen to a California attorney (in pretty much the gobbledygook language of the state bar association):

Private Reproval. The attorney is found culpable (that means guilty) of professional misconduct, but no period of suspension is imposed. The attorney's name is not publicized but he may be required to pass the Professional Responsibility Examination and/or comply with conditions similar to probation.

Public Reproval. The attorney is found culpable of professional misconduct, but no period of suspension is imposed. Attorney's name and imposition of discipline are public.

Involuntary Inactive Enrollment. The attorney is enrolled as an inactive member of the State Bar pursuant to Business & Professional Code Section 6007 and is ineligible to practice law pending further order.

Further Discipline for Failure to Comply with a Previous Order. An attorney may be suspended from practice or disbarred for failure to comply with requirements imposed by the California Supreme Court in prior disciplinary orders.

Interim Suspension Following Criminal Conviction. An attorney who has been convicted of a crime that involves or probably involves moral turpitude may be temporarily suspended from the practice of law pending the finality of his/her conviction and a determination regarding degree of attorney discipline that should be imposed as a result of that conviction.

Resignation with Discipline Charges Pending. The attorney voluntarily resigns as a member of the state bar while disciplinary investigation or proceeding is pending. These disciplinary matters may be reopened if the attorney applies for reinstatement to the practice of law.

Suspension/Probation. The attorney is suspended from the practice of law for a specified period of time. Suspension may include a requirement of compliance with conditions of probation and a period of actual suspension from practice. The attorney may not practice law during a period of actual suspension. The attorney may be required to pass the California Professional Responsibility Examination and/or notify clients and interested parties of the suspension. (Did you catch the "may be required to notify clients"? Your attorney could be suspended at this very moment and you wouldn't know unless you contacted the bar association.)

Disbarment. The attorney's name is stricken from the roster of attorneys by the California Supreme Court and he is ineligible to practice law. Attorney may (there it is again) be required to notify clients and interested parties of the disbarment.

Starting to get the picture? Seems to me an attorney almost has to intentionally mess up and then thumb his nose at the state bar investigators before anything serious happens. And even then, he only "may" have to tell his clients about it.

In fairness, however, the State Bar of California handles a lot of cases and the names of more than a few lawyers show up each month as a matter of public record. Again, we don't know how many of those secret *Private Reprovals* there are, but in a typical month you're likely to see one or two *Public Reprovals*, one or two *Involuntary Inactive Enrollments*, four or five *Suspension/Failure to Pass Professional Responsibility Examinations*, nearly a dozen *Resignations/Charges Pending*, a half dozen or so *Interim Suspensions*, nearly two dozen actual *Suspension/Probations*, and a handful of *Disbarments*.

The *Interim Suspensions* in one particular month involved one attorney being convicted of conspiracy to commit mail fraud and wire fraud. Another was convicted of embezzling property belonging to a bankruptcy estate while he was an officer of the court. Two lawyers were temporarily suspended for being convicted of defrauding the U.S. government by impeding the collection of income taxes. Another was convicted on 40 counts of loitering and peeping and one count of receiving stolen property. And the bar suspended another after his felony conviction of a forcible lewd act committed on a child. Nasty, eh?

In another month, attorneys were temporarily suspended following convictions for business fraud, making a false statement in a bankruptcy petition, and sexual battery. When attorneys are convicted of crimes, they're required to report the conviction to the state bar. A good number of those that fall in the *Suspension/Probation* category are there because they failed to report their convictions.

Or sometimes the convicted lawyer stupidly repeats the crime. Take the case of the lawyer who was convicted of driving under the influence in 1992 and placed on criminal probation. The next year, the fellow had too much to drink, mowed down and seriously injured a pedestrian and then drove off. The district attorney dismissed a count of driving under the influence of alcohol in a deal where the attorney pleaded guilty to felony hit-and-run driving. The state bar suspended him for three years, but stayed (meaning they didn't enforce) the suspension and placed him on probation for three years with a six-month actual suspension.

Or take the case of the attorney who, in 1991, was suspended for two years (with only 30 days of actual suspension) after he was convicted on two counts of battery, two counts of violation of a court order, and one count of unlawful entry. This followed an altercation with his ex-wife. Three years later he pleaded guilty to violating a restraining order and entering her home.

My favorite was the lawyer who celebrated the holidays by going to a bar dressed up as Santa Claus. He danced, he drank and he entertained the ladies. When the bar closed, he asked two of the women he'd been dancing with if they'd give him a ride home. Since some of their friends had acknowledged knowing him—and, of course, because he was Santa Claus—they thought it would be okay to give him a ride. Somewhere along the way, he apparently criticized the way the one woman was driving. She didn't like some of the words he was saying, so she stopped the car and ordered him out. When he wouldn't budge, she pulled what turned out to be a toy gun on him. That angered him so much he grabbed her steering wheel "club" and proceeded to bash the heck out of the interior of her car.

Pretty soon he grabbed her purse and ran, with her chasing after. Some passing police officers couldn't help but notice the sight—Santa running down the median of the boulevard with a purse in hand and its owner at his heels. He pleaded no contest to a public nuisance charge. But this wasn't the first time he found himself behind bars. His criminal file showed he had a history of substance-abuse problems, violent behavior and psychological dysfunction. Matter of fact, the local police already knew him well from past contacts. Seems he'd made some meritless claims and had to face allegations of theft and unlawful possession of a firearm. Once, in fact, he was arrested at a major international airport for trespassing onto the runway and climbing into an open airplane.

Was this enough to have him disbarred? Nope. His one-year suspension was stayed in favor of a year of probation with only 90 days of actual suspension, and more if he fails to give the state bar his current address. And if that goes over two years, he'll be suspended until he proves he's rehabilitated and fit to practice. Oh, and they also ordered him to take the Professional Responsibility Examination.

So I ask you, would any of this stuff matter to you if you were about to plunk down a couple of thousand dollars to someone you expect to handle your legal matters? So far, none of the cases I've described have anything to do with the actual practice of law. Most of the actual suspensions involve cases where lawyers knowingly do things that harm their clients.

The number of ways an attorney can knowingly screw up things for his client is almost limited to your imagination. Here are just a few examples:

An attorney drafted a will for a client and nominated himself as the executor (the person who will represent the estate and be in charge of seeing that everything gets fairly distributed after the client dies). After the client died, he loaned $30,000 of the dead guy's (now the estate's) money to himself and some other clients. He even admitted to the judge he knowingly did it. He paid the money back, but since he also pleaded no contest in criminal court of fraudulent misappropriation of property by a fiduciary (someone trusted to take care of someone else's money), he was disbarred.

Another attorney negotiated a settlement in a medical malpractice case but somehow forgot to tell his client. Even worse, he also forgot to give his client his share of the settlement—instead, he used those funds to pay an expert witness in another case. The state bar suspended him for 30 days.

Then there was the lawyer who took on a personal-injury case but waited an entire year before he filed the actual papers in court. Then another year passed with him taking no further legal action. The client desperately tried to make contact with the attorney, but had no luck. So the client hired another attorney. But the first attorney refused to respond to the request that he officially notify the courts he was off the case. The new attorney filed a complaint with the state bar, but the first attorney ignored the bar also. Finally, after he failed to make several court appearances, a judge found him guilty of contempt of court, fined him and relieved him as counsel for the client. Since he even failed to cooperate with the state bar, they gave him a whopping six-month suspension.

Another attorney agreed to defend a client and a company in a civil action. He didn't do some of the things he was required to do and also refused to allow his client to see the files. Then, the attorneys for the other side filed a motion compelling the first attorney to turn over some information. Neither did he do what he was ordered to do nor did he tell his client about it. Next thing you know the judge awarded more than $350,000 to the plaintiff. And, just like the attorney in the last example, he refused to turn over any files to the client and refused to cooperate with the new attorney. The state bar's action? A suspension of 90 days and an order he pay back the money he didn't earn.

If you can personally visit the state bar offices, plan on spending a few hours looking through any files relating to the attorney you're investigating. It will be time well-spent.

Chapter Four

☑ *Law Schools*

I sent out a carload of little questionnaires to attorneys all over the place and I went and shook hands with a lot of them, too. I thought maybe they could give me some insight into how to check out other attorneys. Bought more than my fair share of coffee and cocktails to get them comfortable so they could talk. The one area that seemed to give me the most trouble was whether the law school an attorney attended had anything to do with how good he ended up as an attorney.

You might be a step ahead of me here. It doesn't take a genius to guess what some of the ones who went to those big, prestigious, ivy-covered colleges back East told me. They'd make you think they should have a corner on the law market. And a few of those who stuck closer to home and went to the state university told me they have a better grip on things—studying in the state they're practicing in and all. And there were a few

who either went to private night school or took correspon-
dence courses. "We had to work a lot harder to get through
school," was a common remark. "And we passed the bar as well
as the other guys."

"I look with a suspicious eye at people who went from high
school to college to law school and then to some big law firm,"
one lawyer told me. "These guys never had any life experience.
They don't have business experience. They've never had to fire
someone. The big law firms hire the graduates from big law
schools because they're image-conscious."

But, surprisingly, most attorneys I talked to don't give a hoot
about the law school.

"School is only marginally important," one attorney told
me. "Most consumers won't know the quality of the school,
even if they find out the name. And many of the lesser-quality
schools graduate excellent attorneys. On the other hand, many
of the better schools graduate lawyers who have little going for
them except that they think they are smart and don't have to
work to earn their reputations."

Another attorney says the type of school someone attends
is really more a measure of how much loot his mom and pop
have than of the guy's character or "street smartness." Indeed,
as he points out, he who passes the bar practices law—regardless of the school.

"My clients need representation by counsel who are experienced in a particular field," said Kevin E. Balfe, "and I do not
believe that a person's academic experience plays any major
role in that regard. I would agree that many people who have
done well in school may have the intelligence necessary to understand a particular legal problem, but lawyering requires much
more than those academic skills." He says he puts more signifi-

cant credence in class ranking.

"If he's not lazy he should have been able to do decently in school. Although I am also aware that some people hate law school, but still end up being good lawyers."

And, while a few attorneys gave weight to both the school and to how the student ranked in class, most pooh-poohed it.

"Class placement is a lot of crap," another lawyer said. "I don't usually care, so long as they have a good reputation among other attorneys in the same field. I am, like anyone else, impressed if I hear that a person was number one at Harvard or something. But short of special information like that, it doesn't matter to me where they went or how they ranked."

Regardless of what the attorneys say, you should consider contacting the law school that graduated the attorney you're investigating. You'll learn the name of the school from the state bar association or the *Martindale-Hubbell Law Directory* at the library.

You should call the school and ask for the records section. Once there, simply say, "I'd like to verify that one of your students graduated." They may ask you why you want to know. You may simply say, "employment verification." It's true. You're either going to be hiring him or firing him, so it's not untrue.

They should be able to verify that he graduated and, if you're at all lucky, the dates he attended, any other major areas of study, the actual degree he received and when, and possibly the school he attended before law school.

It never hurts to check the other degrees or education he may have received. When you call any university, consider calling the actual department in which he was enrolled. For example, he may have majored in political science before he went to law school. By calling the political science department at the university, you may score big. The staff will often go through their rolodexes or card files and give you lots of great information, such as where he lived back then, where he worked, what organizations he belonged to, and any awards he may have won.

It never hurts to check.

Chapter Five

☑️ *Using Public Records*

Don't skip over this chapter. It will probably be the most important one in this book. In fact, a lot of people will buy the book just for all the stuff I've jam-packed into this chapter. The cool thing about the information here is that you don't have to use it just for attorneys. You can use these techniques to check out just about anybody—your boss, your noisy neighbors, your daughter's boyfriend, your husband's girlfriend, your girlfriend's husband—well, you get the picture.

The added bonus is that public records are free and usually you don't have to tell anyone who you are or why you want to see them. And, even better, the person you're snooping into won't have a clue that you or anyone is looking. Now doesn't that make this chapter worth the price of the entire book?

First of all I'd better explain what public records are. They're a pretty big portion of all the paperwork, computer informa-

tion, photographs, videotapes, films and such that the government keeps on file. Because of some laws at the federal and
state levels, we, the people, have a right to check up on our
government to make sure it's doing things right. Since all those
government workers are really our employees, and since they're
shuffling and filing all those papers using our tax dollars, and
since those papers might reflect the way they're doing their
jobs—well then, we have a right to inspect them.

Of course, there are some files that the average Joe shouldn't
be poking into. We certainly don't want people snooping in on
bona fide police investigations. And there's no reason any of us
should be getting the home addresses of government workers.
Trade secrets are allowed to remain secret. Information that
could jeopardize national security is restricted. And things such
as where Exxon is drilling test holes for oil and how much money
you have in federally insured banks—well, those are things
people just shouldn't get their grimy hands on. So they're not
considered public records.

But that still leaves a whole bunch of files you can look at.
And there's enough great stuff available on just about anybody—
especially attorneys—to pretty much tell their life stories.

Get comfortable, because I'm going to overwhelm you with
great sources of information. One thing you may want to make
note of, however, is that the very same information you're finding about that attorney, someone else can find out about you. It
might make you think twice before doing some of the things
that generate public records.

Granted, some of the things you'll learn here may not be
the most relevant when it comes to checking out a lawyer, but
I'm throwing them in anyway for two reasons. First, you really
might want to learn every speck of detail about the scoundrel—

you'll find that having information sometimes makes you feel good. And secondly, this stuff may come in handy for other purposes. For instance, you may have some loud neighbors who can't hear you screaming, "Turn down that dagnabbed music!" over the roar of heavy metal. If they're renters, you can use public records to find out who the owner is and play him a recording of what you must endure. Or, you may want to check out your daughter's new date. Or track down an old army buddy or school chum or old girlfriend.

Now in my little survey of attorneys, a whole bunch of them were downright irate that a client of theirs might be snooping into their public record files.

"What does it matter what the attorney does in his private life?" asked one lawyer friend of mine. "So he's got a nasty divorce. Maybe he's a natural-born fighter. That's exactly who you want fighting for you."

My attorney friend Mark Pollack is, again, in the minority on this issue. "You want a reputable, respected practitioner," he told me. "You don't want a fighter who lacks conflict resolution skills. If you've got a madman who doesn't pay his taxes, the chances are your case is in peril in his hands. The shortest distance between your problem and its resolution could very well be effective compromise. The image of the belligerent barracuda attorney is a TV image."

So don't worry about angering the attorney you're investigating by digging into public records. He'll just have to get over it. And besides, you probably won't be telling him you were looking. The keepers of the files sure won't squeal.

There are public records available at every level of government—townships, cities, counties, special districts, state and federal. You're never going to be able to look at all the public records—there are just too many of them. Some are so obscure you'd never need to look at them. Others aren't worth the trouble of all the digging you'd have to do. For example, you could find out, using public records, which cars had received parking tickets in front of a certain address for the past five years. But since neither the police nor the courts file the tickets by address, you'd have to manually leaf through thousands and thousands of individual citations. Sure, if you're looking to prove some child molester was in your neighborhood on a certain date, it would be worth the effort—but not normally.

What's surprising is just how willing the government officials are to hand you the file. A lot of folks don't realize that it's the job of that clerk to give out files all day long. Most of the time you'll meet no resistance at all. If you approach the clerk in a heavy-handed way, though, that old clerk might just get back at you by making the file disappear or by closing early for lunch. There's never any good reason for going to blows with a clerk who has the files you want. You can't win unless the person wants to help you. Demanding the files is about as futile as trying to snatch a bone out of the mouth of a hungry wolf—you're likely to encounter some stiff resistance.

If someone tells you what you're looking for is not open for public inspection, politely (very politely) tell them you'd like to see the law, memo, ruling or citation that allows them to withhold the particular records. "My boss is going to want to know why I came back empty-handed," is what I usually say. This approach is less confrontational. Many times the clerk is simply withholding the file because no one has ever asked for it before. When he checks with the supervisor or office manager, he often learns that the file is public. You don't have to beat him up for it, though. If you've done the job right, he'll be happy to eventually give you the file—especially because you haven't pulled his chain.

LOCAL RECORDS

I'll start off with the lowest level of government and work my way up. Keep in mind that some states keep files at different levels than other states. I've found that on the East Coast, townships and cities keep a lot more of the records than counties. But as you move west, the counties are more likely to have more of the files.

Like I said, it normally doesn't cost anything to view the records. If you want copies, however, they're going to charge you for them. Sometimes they're as cheap as a nickel a page and other times you could have to shell out a couple of bucks.

At the township or city level, you're likely to find business permits or licenses. The city or town collects a percentage of the revenues of certain businesses—maybe even law firms in your area. Normally, you can find out any of three things: the name of the business, the true owner of the business, and the business address. If you know any one of these three things, the clerk should be able to give you the other two. This can come in handy if the lawyer you're investigating has some other businesses or locations. Just give the clerk the attorney's name and ask what other businesses he's associated with. If he works for a law firm, you might be able to find out who's running the company and what other businesses they're associated with. You will not normally be able to find out how much money they're making or paying out in taxes, but it can't hurt to ask the clerk.

The city or town clerk might also keep some other interesting information on file. Sometimes they keep track of burglar alarms and concealed weapon permits. They'll also keep track of some voting and election information, but I'll be getting to that later.

Another fun file at the city or town level is the building permit. Give the clerk the address of the lawyer and you should be able to look at all the building permits over the years involving that address. Whoever owned the place had to get permits to demolish old buildings, to grade the land, to pour the foundation of the house, to do the plumbing, the electricity, the air conditioning and heating, the carpentry, the roof, the pool and much more. This is a great way of seeing where your money went. The swimming pool could have been built thanks to a really messy divorce. That add-on might have been the result of a good injury case or two.

When you're investigating someone, the building permits are a great way of finding people who had once been inside the house. The names, addresses and phone numbers of all the contractors show up clearly on the building permit. You might want to ask the contractor if he got paid on time. If you're looking into a judge, prosecutor or other government official, you might look to see if their contractor is also doing work for the city or town. This is a great place to discover bribes and kickbacks. It's the old I'll-make-sure-you-get-the-contract-to-paint-city-hall-if-you-give-me-a-break-on-painting-my-own-house game. It happens in towns and cities all over the country, but few people ever look for the evidence.

The secretary of state of one eastern seaboard state recently resigned when a reporter discovered the official was ordering his own staff to do remodeling work on the home of a female employee he was fond of. Turns out he'd helped the "family friend" get hired onto his staff in the first place.

While you're there at the city or township, ask them about animal licensing. You may think this is trivial, but it's one of my favorite places to look. If someone has a pet and treats it well, they can't be too bad a person. On the other hand, anyone who abuses or neglects a little critter deserves to be chained to a tree for a couple of days. At the very least, you'll have one more nugget for your files.

Also at the city or township level you're likely to find a variety of permits to do other things. Some areas require permits to hold yard sales or garage sales. It never hurts to ask the city or town clerk what else is available. Some of the New England states compile all the information about a person or family or address into one big master book. Find the address of the lawyer and you're likely to find out about pets, building permits, business permits, voter affidavits, property tax records, vital records and even vehicle tax records—all in one convenient place. I stopped into a township in New Hampshire and discovered that anyone who decides to move into the area must fill out a big questionnaire that asks for all kinds of information. Get your hands on that sheet and you won't have to do much legwork.

When it comes to voter registration information, property tax information, and birth, marriage and death certificates, you may find them either at the town, city or county level—depending upon what state you're in. Regardless of where you get them, however, these records are among the most useful when you're investigating someone. The next sections cover these areas.

Voter Records

Most states still allow you to view the index of registered voters within a town, city or county (and within some entire states). The index alone should show you where someone lives, how long they've been voting there, their date of birth or age, where they were born, their political persuasion and maybe even their occupation and unlisted phone number. That'll either be indexed in a book form, on microfiche or in a computer database. Once you find the index reference, you may also be able to view the actual affidavit they filled out. This could include even more information, such as Social Security number, description, occupation, phone number, prior address and an original signature. Cool, eh?

No matter at what level of government you find the voting records, you should also ask about campaign-financing statements. Did your lawyer ever run for office? Or maybe contribute to someone else who was running for office? A ballot measure, perhaps? Or maybe he belongs to or contributes to some political action committee (PAC). If that's the case, you can surely inspect the records and see who contributed how much to whom and how the candidate, PAC, or ballot measure committee spent the money. It's a great way to see who's buttering whose bread. In a lot of places, nobody really checks to make sure one particular person isn't contributing more to a candidate than the law allows. You might discover some wrongdoing on the part of your attorney or his buddies seeking political office.

And always remember that campaign-financing statements are also kept on file at the state level for statewide offices, and at the Federal Election Commission for people running for national office.

Also, while you're there, ask if candidates and public officials have to fill out a conflict-of-interest statement. Sometimes it's called a statement of economic interest. This dandy little jewel pops up every so often when some lawyer runs for city attorney or district attorney or county counsel or even for the school board or police commission. If you're lucky enough to find one, you'll have saved yourself a lot of legwork. That's because most people who are required to complete this annual form have to disclose all the property they own, loans they've received, loans they've given out, other income sources, savings accounts, stocks they own, boards they sit on and even gifts they've received. It's certainly worth looking for.

Property Records

Another gold mine of information is also at the town, city or county level. It's the tax assessor. The files at this office give you a pretty good idea about what property the lawyer owns and what it's worth. You can also find out here whether the taxes are paid up. Generally, you can look up the name of the attorney in the alphabetical name index. Once you zero in on the actual tax rolls you'll probably learn the address of the property (the situs address), the official book, page and parcel number, the assessed value of the land and improvements (those are the buildings on the property), any exemptions, some description of the land and the buildings, and usually a reference number that leads you to another office where they keep the actual deed he got when he bought the property. You can also get a copy of the assessor's map that shows his whole neighborhood.

And before you leave the assessor's office, ask them if they also handle the taxes for unsecured property. That refers to big-ticket items that aren't attached to the earth the way the house and lot are—items such as airplanes, big boats, giant computer systems, machinery and a slew of other things the county wants you to pay taxes on. This is a great way to find things that wouldn't otherwise show up in public record. It's quite likely you'll find something here because lawyers like to buy big toys. Who knows, maybe he'll let you go for a ride on the airplane you helped him buy.

If your assessor doesn't keep track of property tax records, scurry on over to the office of the tax collector. You'll find out there if your attorney is paid up.

Just because you found reference to the lawyer's real estate holdings at the assessor's office doesn't mean you should stop. There's an entire other office with even better goodies. In most places it's called the recorder's office. Again, it might be at either the town hall, city hall or at the county courthouse. In your area they might call it the recorder of deeds or something like that.

The recorder's office is filled with great stuff. If you understand why the recorder exists, it's a whole lot easier understanding all the wonderful things you can find there. You see, a long time ago people would sign civil contracts for things and keep a copy for proof. But pretty soon some scoundrels who were a bit more clever than they were honest began altering their copies of documents. Say, for example, someone signed a deed of trust promising to pay $100 a month for some property. All he had to do was add a decimal point and another zero to make his copy read $10.00 a month. Of course, the guy he was paying had an original that showed $100, but when he took his evidence before a judge in civil court, who's to say which of the two documents was altered?

It didn't take long before the powers that be said, "Looks like we can't trust any of you to be civil. From now on, people can bring their original down here to the new recorder's office and he'll make a copy no one can alter." From then on, anyone disputing the validity of any document could zip down to the recorder's office and buy a certified copy of the original.

That's where you come in. You have just as much right to look at all those recorded documents as the next guy. And you're likely to find a whole array of things there. Most of the documents relate to real estate purchases. We'll start there.

Remember when you were at the assessor's office and I told you that you might find some sort of reference number among the other things in the file? Well, the reference number is probably the number the recorder gave to the deed over at the recorder's office. Trust me, it's often a lot quicker finding the number to the deed at the assessor's office than at the recorder's office. That's because the recorder usually only handles a document one time. He checks to make sure the signature is bona fide, makes sure the recording fee is paid, and makes sure any transfer taxes are paid. Then he simply puts a consecutive number on the top of it, copies it onto microfilm or microfiche and sends the original back to whoever requested the recording. The only information on the document he cares about is the number he gave it, the date he recorded it, the type of document it is, and the names of the people involved in the transaction—usually the grantor and the grantee. The grantor is the person granting the document and the grantee is the person receiving the document. The recorder doesn't care what else is written on the document. Heck, I could make up a deed granting you the Lincoln Memorial or O'Hare International Airport and the local recorder would record it—as long as I signed it in front of a notary public, as long as I paid the recording fee, and as long as I paid any transfer taxes. Beyond that, the recorder doesn't care.

That's important to keep in mind. Just because the deed (or any other document) has been recorded doesn't mean the information on it is real. Most the time it is, but there are some folks out there who delight in tricking people into paying for property that belongs to someone else.

The seller of a house or building or piece of property signs a document known as a deed and gives it to the buyer. If the buyer has half a brain, he'll rush down to the recorder and have it recorded. Otherwise, the seller could make up another deed and sell the same property to someone else. Don't laugh, it happens. That's why you're almost assured to find the deed at the recorder's office.

The deed has a lot of information on it, but it's amazing some of the obvious information that may not show up on it. What you will find is the name of the grantor (in this case the person selling or releasing the property), the grantee (the buyer or receiver), the legal description of the property, the date the transaction took place, and the signatures of the seller (grantor) and of the notary public who witnessed the signature. What you may not find is the address of the property and the sale price. But there are usually ways of getting this information.

Folks are usually reluctant to describe the property on a deed by using an address. That's because things change with a piece of property—at least in the way it's used. What's a farm one day with some rural route number as an address may become a development of single-family houses the next day. Someone might mow down three or four houses on a block and build condominiums. In each case, the address will change. So a long time ago they decided to use a legal description instead of an address. The legal description is a set of words that describe the exact location and boundaries of the property. The words might tell you where the property is in relation to some fixed objects such as a mountain, a rock or some other point on earth that's not likely to move. Or, the legal description might relate to a map some developer made up years ago when he turned the farmland into streets and houses. Back then he may have drawn up a tract map showing where he plans on dividing up his property. He may have even named the tract after himself—say, the Johnson Tract. He may have broken the property up into sections and then broken the sections up into blocks and the blocks into actual lots. He numbered the sections, blocks and lots and then filed the tract map with the city or county recorder. So if you bought one of the houses there, the legal description on your deed could read something like:

Lot 4 of Block 2 of Section 1 of the Johnson Tract as filed with the county recorder on Pages 215 and 216 of Book 2901 on June 14, 1942. Instead of being called the Johnson Tract, the recorder may have given it a unique number—Tract 3499 or something like that.

Any changes in land use would still reflect that original tract map. If you bought your neighbor's property and then sold both as one big lot, the legal description would simply read:

Lots 4 and 5 of Block 2 of Section 1 of the Johnson Tract as filed with the county recorder on Pages 215 and 216 of Book 2901 on June 14, 1942.

It can get more detailed if you sell less than a complete lot. Then it might describe the actual line "running in a northerly direction beginning 50 ft. east of the southwest corner of Lot 5, Block 2, Section 1 and ending 50 ft. east of the northwest corner of Lot 5, Block 2, Section 1..."

The thing to understand here is that the legal description is a set of words that specifically tells you where the property is in relation to something somewhere.

However, you might just find the property address listed right there in the deed, but for another reason. There is a block on many blank deed forms that says, "When recorded, send the original to:" Another says, "Send tax statements to:" Either of these could show the address of the property, but you can't immediately be sure. They could both be addresses of accountants, lawyers, business offices or whatever. But don't despair; I guarantee you'll find the address soon. It may just show up on another document.

About the purchase price? Even though it may not be spelled out on the deed, you still might find a clue. Many recorders generate a lot of revenue by charging a documentary transfer tax. This tax is usually levied on the people recording deeds to property. Usually they have to pay an amount based on the total selling price of the property. Some places charge $1 transfer tax for every $1,000 of the sale price. The amount of transfer tax paid is usually typed or written on the deed before it's recorded. So if you see that someone paid $100 in documentary transfer taxes, then you can pretty easily figure out that the sale price was $100,000. It's a match thing. You just multiply the transfer tax paid by 1,000. In California, most counties charge $1.10 per $1,000 of the sale price. I think they do it so it's not as easy to compute. What I do is divide the transfer tax by .0011. What results from the division problem is the sale price of the property. So if someone paid $220 in transfer taxes in California I'd divide $220 by .0011 and end up with $200,000 as the sale price. Pretty cool, huh?

But if all else fails, there's probably some sheet on the wall or at the recorder's desk that quickly translates documentary transfer tax paid into sale price. Just ask.

I really doubt, however, that someone could come up with that much money to buy property without borrowing a big chunk of it. And when someone borrows money to buy a house, or otherwise uses the house as collateral for a loan, you're likely to find a deed of trust or trust deed on file with the recorder. Most recorders number the documents they record consecutively as they come in. On January 1st, the first document they record will have a number of 000001. The tenth will be 000010. The 157th will be 000157 and so on. Usually the people who actually bring in real estate documents for recording bring them in one big bunch. So what you'll soon discover is that the number given the trust deed is one higher than the number given the deed. If there's a second trust deed, its number is one higher than the first deed of trust and so on. In places that file them using this system, it's easy to find the trust deeds—right behind the deeds. In some offices, however, they make up a separate file and numbering system for different types of documents. Be sure you ask a clerk to explain the system they use at that office.

So that you can more easily find specific recorded documents, the recorder usually makes up alphabetical indices (that's plural for index). Sometimes there's one index for all the grantors and a separate index for the grantees. It's always a good idea to look up the attorney's name in both indices. If he's buying a house, he'll be a grantee of the deed (he's receiving it) and the grantor of the deed of trust (he's granting the promise to pay the lender). Starting to get the idea? It's all about which direction the piece of paper goes.

So, a deed is a piece of paper someone signs that gives someone else interest in property. The deed of trust is a different bird all together. The owner of the property (either a new buyer or a longtime owner who's using his house as collateral to borrow money) is saying to the lender, "Hey, pal, if I don't pay you the money I owe you under the terms of this deed of trust, you can sell the property, and from the money it gets, keep what I owe you plus a whole wagon load of fees and penalties and such."

Trust deeds are a lot fatter than deeds. While a deed is normally only a page in length, the deed of trust can run a dozen pages or more. But don't let that throw you. What you generally need to know is on the first page and the last page. Everything in between is just a bunch of legal jargon that pretty much protects the lender and hangs the borrower out to dry if he doesn't pay on time.

A trust deed almost always tells you three important things: the names of all the folks involved in the loan, the amount of the loan, and the address of the property in question. It will also have the legal description, but you already got that off the deed.

Just to confuse you, they give a whole bunch of different names to the people involved in a real estate loan. The owner of the house is also, of course, the borrower. But they sometimes won't call him that on the trust deed. They're more likely to call him the trustor. I know what you're thinking, he's not the one doing the trusting. Just accept it. He's also the one granting the document (or promise to pay) so he's also the grantor. At least this title makes sense.

The person or bank or finance company actually lending the money, and ultimately benefiting by receiving the payments, is the beneficiary. And, of course the person or organization lending the money is the lender. They're also the recipient of the promise to pay, so you'd find them also filed as the grantee. Are you confused yet? Were you expecting the lender to also be the trustee? Read on.

The trustee on a trust deed is often a third party. It's usually some finance company, title company or other company whose job it is to administer the loan—you know, send out the bills, collect the money, keep track of what's owed and all that stuff. It gets paid by the lender to manage the loan. They're all going to be labeled on the deed of trust, so it's a good idea to know the players.

Again, the borrower is the grantor and the trustor. The lender is the grantee and the beneficiary. The company processing and administering the loan is the trustee. The first baseman lives next to the guy who smokes Camels. The guy across the street has two more kids than the pitcher and there are no Chevy owners in the outfield. Got it?

You'll always see the amount of the loan clearly typed in, usually on the front page of the deed of trust. Remember, this isn't the total purchase price unless it's one of those very rare instances where a bank is willing to finance the entire amount of the sale. This is just the amount the buyer borrowed—from at least one lender.

So now you've figured out the sale price from the deed and you can read the amount of one big loan from some lender. Chances are the amount of the loan is less than what you computed the sale price to be. Example: you compute the sale price to be $300,000. You look at the deed of trust and see that it's in the amount of $220,000. That leaves a difference of $80,000, right? What is it? Could it be that the buyer gave the seller $80,000 as a down payment and financed the rest? Sure. But that's a lot of cash to have on hand for a down payment—even for a lawyer.

I'd take a look at the very next consecutive document at the recorder's officer. First there was the actual deed. That was followed by the first deed of trust. Could there be a second deed of trust? If there is one, it's likely to be the very next recorded document. It could be a deed of trust between the buyer and a different financial institution, between him and a relative, or even between him and the seller. In other words, the seller could be carrying a second mortgage on the property for, say, $20,000. That would mean that of the $300,000 the property sold for, the seller got $220,000 directly from the lender in the first deed of trust and $60,000 in the form of a cash down payment from the buyer. The seller would then receive monthly payments from the buyer, with interest, until the second deed of trust in the amount of $20,000 is paid off.

It's possible there could be a third, fourth or fifth deed of trust on file—or even more. It's up to you to look for them all and account for all the money. If that buyer should flake out and not make all the payments, the house would be sold at auction. Then the holder of the first deed of trust would get first grabs at the money, then the holder of the second, the third, etc. As you can see, if you're further down on the trust deed food chain, you have a greater chance of starving.

One last, but very important, piece of information on a deed of trust is that all-important property address. Although they'll surely provide the legal description, they'll almost always print the actual address of the property. When it comes to making sure someone knows they're obligated to pay for what they bought, you'd better spell it out too clearly.

Another common real estate document is called the reconveyance. When the borrower pays off a deed of trust, it's no longer in effect. You can't remove any documents from the recorder's public file, so the lender must file a notice that says, "Hey, everybody. That old loan has been paid off. Ignore that deed of trust from back a few years ago."

Don't expect the reconveyance to have too much detail. At most, it will name the borrower and the lender and make reference to the number the recorder gave the original deed of trust. It's up to you to find the reference number on the deed of trust and then go back and see which loan was paid off.

Keep in mind now that people don't usually go around buying houses unless they've recently sold one. This isn't like Monopoly. In real life you've got to sell off Baltic Avenue at a profit to afford Virginia Ave. People don't usually pass "Go" quickly enough to keep buying stuff without selling something. In fact, when you see indications of a big down payment—like the $60,000 down payment in the example above—you should look carefully among all those deeds and deeds of trust for a reconveyance. Many times they'll be right there in the same sequence.

Other times they'll be filed within a month or so of the new purchase.

Now, if you want to find out what that lawyer you're investigating is really worth, spend a day or two in the recorder's office and get copies of every document you can find with his name on it. If you do a thorough enough job, you'll be able to make up sort of a balance sheet on him. You'll find the deed to his first house and the trust deeds involved. Make note of what the price was and how much he borrowed. Then look a few years later in the files and you'll undoubtedly find him selling his property and buying something else. Make note of the sale price by looking at the deed he granted to the buyer. Look for reconveyances and then subtract the original loan amounts from the money the new buyer paid. That'll tell you how much the lawyer made in profit from the sale. There was a time when real estate increased in value while it just sat there. Those were the good old days.

Let's go back to our earlier scenario. Remember the lawyer apparently put $60,000 down on that $300,000 property he bought? Well, maybe by looking at older documents you'll find that he sold a house for $75,000 more than the original purchase price. That gave him enough for a down payment and some extra cash to pay the movers.

I was once giving a public records research demonstration to a bunch of police investigators. One of them told me I could check him out using public records (technically I didn't need his permission, but since he was carrying a loaded gun and all...). I first went to the assessor's office and was astounded to find him living in a mansion on a hill overlooking the ocean. It had cost him nearly $1.5 million. On a cop's salary? No way. I dug in deeper—looking for the sweet smell of corruption—and was disappointed to learn the truth.

When I went way back to when he was 19 or so, I found
that he had invested a few hundred dollars in a couple of brush-
covered hillside lots miles from the nearest road. The lots were
in a place that would later be called Rolling Hills Estate—now
one of the most expensive neighborhoods in the United States.
He had sold them when developers were buying up any land
that could, one day, be a development. With his very big profits,
he bought an older house in another part of the Palos Verdes
Peninsula. Within a few years, the L.A. yuppies discovered his
ocean-view neighborhood and gobbled up the house at another
huge profit. Records showed he wisely invested in the area that
would next become prime territory for the rich. With the profits
from that house, he and his wife built the mansion on the hill.
And to think I put the money I saved into a 1961 Ford Galaxy.
Damn! Deeds, trust deeds and reconveyances, as you can see,
give you a pretty good idea of how much money someone has
wrapped up in real estate.

There are some other real estate-related documents you'll
surely encounter at the recorder's office. Every so often you'll
see a critter called a quit claim deed. Notice I didn't say quick
claim deed. That's how a lot of folks say it—and it kind of makes
sense, because someone's usually in some kind of a hurry about
the time they need to use it. You'll see it a lot when people are
getting divorced, getting married or getting a loan on some
piece of property. The thing that makes it different from a regu-
lar deed (grant deed, individual grant deed, corporate grant
deed—they're all deeds) is that a quit claim deed doesn't so
much transfer specific interest in something as it gives up interesting in something—and that interest isn't spelled out. I know
you're scratching your head and thinking this is a great time to
put this book down and go get something to eat. You know
you shouldn't! Stick with me and feed your brain.

Here's a "for instance." Suppose you and your wife want to

split up. You agree that she gets the house. You're both currently on that deed you got when you bought the house. You could pay to have someone write up a deed specifying that you are transferring your one-half, undivided interest in said property to your wife, who will soon not be your wife, who previously held a one-half, undivided interest in said property but now will own 100% of the property. (I'm not even sure if I got that right.) With a quit claim deed, you're saying, "Hey, whatever my interest was, she now has it." You're kind of leaving it up to someone else to research the old deed to see what your interest once was.

Whether your interest was 100%, 50%, 10% or even if you only held the mineral rights, the quit claim deed reads the same way. In fact, a person doesn't have to have any interest at all and they still might sign a quit claim deed.

Another for instance: Paul and Paula are very much in love and know they'll be together forever. Paul owns a mountain cabin on a two-acre lot that his dad left him. Paul dearly loves Paula, but there's this tiny voice of reason in him that isn't sure the marriage won't end in divorce and that Paula will claim that cabin as community property. So Paul wisely buys some 20-year-old Chablis, lights a few candles, pours Paula a drink and says, "Sweetheart, precious, pumpkin, would you sign this for me, please? It's nothing important. Another glass of wine?"

Fast forward a few years. Paul and Paula are divorcing and not following the advice I gave in Chapter One. It's an all-out ground war. Her attorney stands up in court and says, "Your honor, my client demands the mountain cabin." Before the judge can even blink, Paul's attorney whips out a certified copy of that old quit claim deed.

"Oh, we'd love to, your honor," says the lawyer, "but Paula

was kind enough to release her interest in that property before they were even married. So sorry."

You might also see a quit claim deed when someone's trying to get a loan on their property, but there's someone's name on the deed who, maybe, has crummy credit or who doesn't earn enough money to qualify for the loan. The lender might insist that the name be removed from the title (deed). This happened to me when I went to refinance my house. When I had bought it, years ago, I couldn't qualify on my own, so my mother co-signed for me. That means she teamed up with me to get the loan. Her income and credit combined with my income and credit allowed me to get the original loan. However, when I went to refinance the house a dozen years later, things were different. I was making more money than before, but my mother had since retired. Her income was now a whole lot less than before. The lender would only loan money to me—not to both of us. That meant my mother had to sign a quit claim deed that would release her interest in the property to me.

Sometimes the same thing will happen when a single man owns his own house and then gets married. In some states, the bride automatically has a claim on half the value of the house—community property and all. If the husband wants to refinance his house, the lender may decide to lend only to him and not to them as a couple. In this case, she would have to sign a quit claim deed that releases to him any potential interest she may have received by saying "I do." But again, her name was never on any deed in the first place.

On the other hand, a quit claim deed can appear worthless, but, in reality, have some real value. Henry, for example, sold his farm 30 years ago to some developer who built a condominium complex. Then, 30 years later he signs a quit claim deed that releases his interest in the farm property to his grandson. Ridiculous, you say? He sold it 30 years ago. Remember, the quit claim deed doesn't specify what the interest is. The only way to determine if the quit claim deed has any value is to research all past deeds involving Henry and the farm. You might discover that when Henry sold the farm, he specifically retained the mineral rights. Now, with the signing of the quit claim deed, Henry releases to his grandson his interest in the farm—all the mineral rights.

The fact is, there's no one document or file that tells you who really owns what, when it comes to real estate. That's why no lender will lend any money for any real estate deal without insisting a qualified researcher go through all the deeds and trust deeds and reconveyances and all. The lender wants to make darned sure the person selling the property really owns it in the first place. These researchers work for title insurance companies. Title insurance companies provide two main services. First, they send their researchers to the recorder's office to make sure the seller really owns the property in the first place and, second, they actually insure their research work. If their researchers screwed up and missed the fact that the seller didn't really have a clear title to the property, the title company is supposed to reach in its corporate pocket and pay its customer, the buyer, for the company's screw-up.

When you go down to the recorder's office, you'll be rubbing elbows with a lot of title company people doing their jobs. They can be pretty helpful at times if you don't bug them too much. I've been in some recorder's offices where the title company people think they own the office—where they wouldn't even tell you your fly was open, much less help you interpret documents. But, for the most part, they'll be helpful if you're halfway decent to them. I find it useful to always have at least one contact at a title company. That way I have someone I can call in a pinch to check his company's computer listings. You see, the bigger title companies will buy copies of every document recorded and then computerize much of the information on the document. Then they build great computer programs that make it easy for them to find documents they need to view. They, for example, can often call up a particular address in their computer and have it print out the document numbers of everything relating to that address. The recorder usually can't do that.

There are more documents you need to know that relate to real estate. If someone doesn't pay their mortgage payment on time, the lender may record a notice of default. This is kind of a public "hear ye, hear ye" notice. "Hear ye! Joe and Jody Jerkface are behind on their mortgage payments. Don't let them say we didn't warn them—here it is, recorded in black and white. If they don't pay, we're going to sell their house right out from under them." If the borrowers get caught up (which includes not only paying the back payments, but also a huge attorney's fee they agreed to pay when they signed the deed of trust they never bothered to read), the lender will record a notice that cancels the notice of default.

If the borrowers don't pay up on time, the lender will probably record a notice of sale. Now it's getting scary for the borrowers. This notice says, "Hear ye, hear ye! Joe and Jody Jerkface still haven't paid up. If any of you folks out there with the cash want to buy their house for a song, show up on the courthouse steps next month with cash in hand. It could be yours. That is, of course, unless the Jerkfaces wake up and pay up."

Again, if the borrowers pay up (and pay even bigger attorney's fees) the lender will record a notice canceling the notice of sale. If it actually sells, the new owner will record his new deed.

You might find some type of attachment filed at the recorder's office. This comes about when a homeowner isn't paying money he owes to someone. The debtor can slap a lien on the property. This pretty much says, "Hear ye, hear ye! Joe and Jody Jerkface owe me some money and I'm attaching the outstanding debt to their house. If anybody out there tries to buy the house from them, you'll have to pay me the money they owe me before you give them anything."

There are various kinds of liens. If the homeowner hires a contractor to put a new roof on the house and then doesn't pay, the contractor may place a mechanic's lien on the property. When you see a mechanic's lien, it usually indicates either the homeowner is a complete flake or there is some kind of a dispute between the homeowner and the contractor. It could be that the homeowner is refusing to pay for the work until the contractor does it right.

Government agencies like to go the lien route. You might find a lien on property placed there by the Internal Revenue Service because the homeowners failed to pay some taxes. This will certainly give you some insight into the finances of the attorney you're checking out. The lien notice will tell you the Social Security number of the attorney and spouse, the amount of taxes they owe, and the tax year in which they're delinquent. Keep in mind that this might indicate that there's some action taking place in U.S. Tax Court. Those files are open to the public and will give you a rare glimpse into someone's personal tax file.

State tax collectors, assessors and others may also file liens on the property of people who haven't paid their due taxes or fees or fines. In each case, the lien may make reference to cases on file with other agencies.

When you find a lien, always look forward in time to see if the homeowner ultimately paid off the debt. If he did, you'll find that the lien holder recorded a release of lien. I've tracked some really flaky people who have had their properties attached six, seven or eight times.

Sometimes disputes between two or more parties over interest in real estate will end up being resolved in civil court. When a judge or jury finally decides who owns what, they'll record a court document called an abstract of judgment. This lets anyone interested in buying the property know who the real owners are.

Keep your eyes peeled for a document called a power of attorney. This is where someone gives another person (not necessarily an actual attorney) permission to handle some transaction on their behalf. Could be, for instance, that Fred is leaving the country for a couple of months but has a house up for sale. He might give power of attorney to a friend or relative that would allow the other person to sign on behalf of Fred. The power of attorney will almost always specify exactly what the other person can do. It might read, for example, "I, Fred Scuffheel, hereby authorize Steve Kneescrape to sign on my behalf regarding the sale of the property at 123 Green Street, Hometown, U.S.A."

Sometimes the power of attorney can lead you to interest in property that's held through some sort of a limited partnership. You see, sometimes people join with a bunch of other investors to buy a big apartment building or something. The deed is in the name of the limited partnership. In many states, the names of the limited partners are not a matter of public record. That's one of the reasons people like limited partnerships—it keeps their assets hidden. But they occasionally slip up by giving power of attorney to either a lawyer or to the general partner (whose name is a matter of public record) empowering that person to sign documents relating to the purchase of the property. While the name of the limited partner will not show up on the deed, it will show up on the power of attorney. And the power of attorney almost always is recorded.

Normally, on the last page, you'll find the actual signatures of the parties to a recorded document. Before the recorder records a document, he insists all signatures be notarized. That means a person commissioned by the state (a notary public) must witness the signature and certify that it's really the signature of the person who signed it. That means the notary has to swear he's known the person signing for a heckuva long time or he must actually check the driver's license or other identification to be sure. In some states this can be a great way to get more information. If you take a copy of the recorded document to the notary public who witnessed the signature, he must show you the stuff he wrote in his notary's log book about the signing. It will often show the name, address, phone number and driver's license number of the person signing the document. In some states, the notary is actually required to take a thumb print from the person signing.

But how do you find the notary public? You're already at the recorder's office. I like to check to see if the notary might have recorded some type of protection bond. If he did, you'll find the address and phone number of the notary right there on the recorded copy of the bond. If you don't find it there, check with your city or county clerk. They often keep listings of every notary in their jurisdiction. The secretary of state might also keep track of all the notaries in the state.

You're probably starting to notice that there are a lot more than just real estate documents on file at the recorder. You're likely to find various kinds of bonds, public notices, contracts between two or more parties, and others. Some veterans take their discharge papers to the recorder so that they can easily pick up certified copies in the future. It's a lot easier to get a copy from the recorder than it is to deal with the Veteran's Administration or the National Personnel Records Center.

Vital Records

Not far from where everyone voluntarily records deeds and things, you're going to find a desk or counter where they record vital statistics—birth, marriage and death certificates. These aren't filed voluntarily—the law requires it. Before I go any further, I should tell you that, in many states, the average Joe can't view these documents or the index. So don't start writing me angry letters when they slam the door in your face. Golly, if I had my way, everything would be open and available. But more and more, yesterday's advocates of free speech and openness in government and all have reaped small fortunes selling water beds or whatever and are now worried about the poor people finding out where they live and work.

One of the very reasons the files were traditionally open was so that people could find out who their parents and grandparents are. People have a right to know that their fiancé isn't already married to someone else. Some states will allow access to records after 50 or 75 years. A lot of good that does when you want to find out if you're the only wife your husband has. Don't laugh—it happens all the time.

If your state does allow you to view and buy copies of the records, you'll find the records at the state capital as well as at the city or county level. Again, the farther west you go, the more likely the records will be at the county level.

There's a lot of good information on a birth certificate. If you're looking at the birth certificate of the attorney you're investigating, you'll find out his parents' names, their places of birth, their address at the time, their professions, places of employment at the time, the doctor who delivered the future lawyer, and an indication of whether the mother had given birth before.

I've found that I can learn some interesting stuff by looking at the birth certificates of someone's children. In particular, you can find fairly recent information about the children's parents. It's a great way to find out where the attorney's spouse works, the mother's maiden name, maybe even where the attorney used to work, his current address and, of course, the place of birth of both parents.

Marriage certificates are also fun. They'll give the bride's maiden name, the home and work addresses of both parties at the time, their occupations, their dates and places of birth, their parents' names and birthplaces, and the all-important witnesses. Most states require two witnesses to the wedding—usually the best man and the maiden of honor. Usually, these two names show up on the marriage certificate along with their addresses and signatures. This can be of great use if you find the marriage certificate of a now-divorced attorney. Here's what you do: If the lawyer was the groom, you should track down the woman who stood up for the bride. The ex-wife may be reluctant to speak out against her ex-hubby—child support, alimony and all. However, it's very likely the best friend of the bride would love to tell you all the rotten things about the guy who made her friend so miserable. Really. It works.

In some states (California is one) couples who have been living together can get what's called a confidential marriage. There's no blood test required, no waiting period and, so that the couple won't be criticized for having lived in sin, the record is sealed and kept from public view. Why, the nerve of them!

Believe it or not, death certificates can be useful. No, not the death certificate of the person you're checking out—but maybe his father or grandfather. Someone once said, "where there's a will, there's a relative." That's why the death certificate is important—it leads you to relatives. It could be that some other family member was the informant on the death certificate. This would be the person who provided all the information about the decedent that shows up on the death certificate. But even if that's not the case, the death certificate alerts you to the possibility that there is a probate case on file in a nearby court. A probate file can provide the names of other family members, as well as lists of liabilities and assets. I'll tell you how to find that later.

There are now quite a few companies that offer the grantor/grantee index or the vital records index (or both) on CD-ROM or on-line. Some of the larger on-line services are Lexis–Nexis, (800) 543-6862; Dataquick, (619) 455-6900; and CDB Infotek, (800) 427-3747. Don't be surprised if you see some of these indices on the Internet. A great place to begin is a website called All-In-One. It links you to some of the best public record and specialty databases on the Net. Its computer address is http://www.albany.net/allinone/.

A new service is being offered on the Internet by the people at Merlin Data Publishing Corporation, (800) 367-6646. The folks there say they'll provide millions of public record listings for a small search fee.

Fictitious Name Statements

Fictitious name statements don't exist everywhere. In some areas they're called assumed names. Basically, when a legal entity (person, partnership, corporation, trust, etc.) uses any name other than their legal name, they must publish the names of the true owners so all the consumers know who's really behind the company. "Hear ye, hear ye! Sucky Vacuum Cleaner Repair is really a fictitious name. Its true owner is really a person named Patrick Prunepainter." That simple. The proof of publication and the original statement form go on file at the office of either the county clerk or the city clerk. You can usually look up the company using the true name or the fictitious name.

Although most law firms are either partnerships or corporations, it's not a bad idea to see if your attorney might have filed a fictitious name statement. It's common for companies to first operate as a fictitious name company and then, when they're more successful, incorporate.

COURT RECORDS

Criminal Court

After you've checked with the bar association (Chapter Three), the next most important area to check is the court system. The most telling information about an attorney will show up in criminal court, civil court, family court, bankruptcy court or probate court.

Criminal cases, of course, involve some government agency claiming a person or corporation committed a crime. The penalty could be fines, jail time, prison time, community service, probation or any combination of the above.

You might find criminal records at any level of government. If your state has them, first check the justice court. It's usually associated with the jurisdiction of a town or city. Then check at the county courts, state courts and U.S. District Court.

At the lowest level of court you're likely to find cases involving infractions, misdemeanors or even some felonies. This could include major and minor traffic violations, petty theft, violations of city codes (e.g., not licensing a pet), driving under the influence of drugs or alcohol, possessing, using or selling drugs, failure to appear in court—a whole bunch of possibilities.

The countywide court should handle just about all the crimes that are worth arresting someone for. Even on nasty felonies (murder, rape, robbery, kidnapping, burglary, etc.), the defendant will probably first appear before a justice of the peace or a municipal court judge to make a plea, and possibly to go through a preliminary hearing. That's where the judge decides if a crime probably occurred and if it looks pretty much like the defendant is dirty.

Not much happens at state courts except for appeals. The U.S. District Court, however, is a place where you might find some gold. Usually people appear in federal criminal court because they broke some specific federal law or they ripped someone off in another state or they violated someone's civil rights. There are hundreds of possibilities. But because federal crimes are often more sophisticated or are much larger in scale, it's not uncommon to see those clever attorneys there as defendants.

At almost any court you visit, there should be a name index you can look through. If you can't look it up directly, the friendly clerk should be able to do it for you. In most places you should be allowed to view at least part of the case file. Look for a document called the complaint. That will declare that the people of your state are charging the defendant with some crime.

Each state differs, but you're likely to find some dandy documents. The arrest report will be the original arresting document and it may include the details of the arrest, identifying information about the defendant (including addresses, phone numbers, employers, and more), names, address and phone numbers of victims or witnesses, and a dialogue the arresting officer wrote that describes what went down.

Every once in a while you'll find a criminal history, or rap sheet. This is a computerized listing of all the guy's prior arrests in either that city, county, state or across the entire United States. In many states the rap sheet is illegal to view or copy, so if you see it in the file, quietly go to some corner and start writing the stuff down before the clerk realizes he forgot to remove it. When in doubt, transcribe.

There might be a separate sheet of paper for each thing that happened in court. These can be difficult to read and understand, but the clerk will usually tell you what happened each time the guy appeared in court. Sometimes the defendant or the victim will flood the judge with letters saying what an angel or rascal the defendant is. Don't believe much of what you read. It's a lot like politicians—if they're supporting another candidate, the guy can do no wrong. But if they oppose the same dude in another election, you'll see the picture of Satan. But these letters can provide a list of the defendant's friends and foes.

Also keep your eyes open for transcriptions of court proceedings, declarations, search warrants and lists of exhibits. Ultimately, there should be some sheet in there that reflects the judge or jury's verdict. Another document should outline the sentence.

There should even be a record of what prison or jail facility the defendant visited and the name of the probation officer or parole officer.

Keep in mind that to find a particular arrest, you must check at the county where the crime occurred. This can be tough if there are a lot of places your subject frequents. I've had good luck calling the state's corrections department at the state capital. They're usually allowed to give out quite a bit of information about their inmates. This could include the case number, the county where the trial took place, the dates and locations of incarceration, release date and the name of a parole officer.

Civil Court

Civil cases pop up when one party or entity (could be a person, a company, an organization, an association or even a government agency) sues another party or entity in court. Almost always the suing party claims it's been damaged and is hoping a judge or jury will make the other party pay some outrageous amount of money.

It's a great place to explore because usually one or more of the parties involved is really angry. And when they get angry, they say and do some pretty stupid things. Most importantly, they inadvertently air all their dirty laundry in open court. They often don't realize that everything they say or do in open court shows up in the case file. And anyone can look at the file. Nifty!

The level of court someone takes their case to is directly related to the amount of money they're asking for in damages. What's interesting, however, is how the level of anger seems to be in reverse proportion to the level of court. What that means to you is that the first place you should look is the small claims court. That's where Average Joe represents himself and takes his petty dispute in front of Judge Wapner or some similar learned judge or commissioner. Usually, neither party is allowed to bring in an attorney. And there are limits on the damages one can claim. Could be as high as $5,000 and as low as $500. It depends on the local economy.

But what makes small claims court such a gold mine is that, quite often, the winner really doesn't win. Either the judge hears the evidence and rules in favor of the plaintiff or the defendant doesn't show up and the plaintiff wins by default. But the plaintiff often learns there are lots of ways the defendant can hide and protect his assets. And that can make it next to impossible to collect anything. The result is a victorious, but very angry, plaintiff.

Find the angry plaintiff who sued your attorney, won, but couldn't collect and you'll find a first-class ally. Once I was having a devil of a time locating a particular sleazeball attorney. He had an unlisted phone number, didn't vote, didn't own property in his own name, and used a driver's license with an old address. Finally, I visited the small claims court and found one lone case where he was the defendant. I made a call to the plaintiff in the six-year-old suit. I asked him if he remembered an attorney named so-and-so.

"You bet I know him," he snapped back. "I won a $700 judgment against the son of a bitch six years ago but the bastard never paid me."

"Well, do you know where he is now?" I asked.

"You bet I know where he is. I've been tracking the creep for the past six years. I can tell you where he's living now, what he's driving, where his kids go to school, where his wife gets her hair done, and who visits him. Do you want to know about his extramarital affair? I'm going to hound that bastard till the day one of us dies."

You may not be as lucky as I was, but don't be afraid to contact his enemies. The case file should have a descriptive explanation of the nature of the complaint, the names and addresses of both parties and, at the very least, a copy of the judgment. Be sure to look for his name in both the plaintiff and defendant (sometimes called respondent) index. It's possible the attorney is out suing poor, innocent folks.

In larger civil suits you'll find more available information. There will almost always be a complaint in some form or another. Sometimes it's typed out nicely in paragraph form—other times it's actually a form that's been checked off. It generally specifies information that shows that this is the right court. It identifies all the parties and then, about four numbered paragraphs in, says, "On or about..." That's where you want to be looking. It'll tell about maybe your attorney and the other party agreeing to do something, or signing a contract, or maybe that one of them was in a particular place when something happened. Following that paragraph, there will be others that describe what went wrong and what the plaintiff wants in return for all that loss and suffering and all. At the end of the complaint it might also include actual copies of contracts, credit reports, loan applications and other key exhibits.

Typically, the next thing you'll find is the answer to the complaint. This is where the defendant (or respondent) goes down the list of numbered paragraphs in the complaint and either confirms or denies the allegations. From there, the case can go just about anywhere. This is where attorneys really shine. They can drag out a simple dispute for years—even decades. So to try explaining the myriad of papers and motions and documents they're capable of filing would take up volumes. The best you can do, really, is to go through each document that's been filed and look for things that might jump out and seem important to you.

You might want look for exhibits. If they're not included or listed, ask the clerk if there may be some. Because exhibits can be pretty bulky, they are often stored in another room. If you don't ask for them, they won't usually volunteer them. The exhibits are commonly transcriptions of depositions (out of court, but under oath testimony) or interrogatories (lengthy questionnaires either side may require the other side to complete).

If you get your hands on an interrogatory your attorney had to complete, you've just hit a grand slam home run. These things get into so much detail it will make you never want to file a lawsuit in your life. If you thought that suing someone who sideswiped your car would require you to itemize every time and place you ever drank a beer or every person who ever rode in your car or other silly and personal things, it might make you think twice about suing. That's one of the reasons attorneys like to use them—it makes the plaintiff feel quite uncomfortable—maybe uncomfortable enough to cause him to back down from the suit.

One important thing to retrieve from the file is the name and phone number of the opposing attorneys. They're usually happy to talk about the case. You never know, they may be representing someone with a complaint similar to the one you may have against the attorney you're investigating. They may also help put you in touch with their client. It could save you doing a public record search to find him yourself.

Family Court

It may have a different name where you are. It might be attached to the countywide civil court or it might be a standalone court. Regardless, family court is going to handle mainly child custody matters and divorces.

When it comes to major league mudslinging, give me a good divorce file any day. There's nothing that compares. I'll never understand how two people who so passionately loved each other can hate each other with equal passion. It's astounding how much nasty stuff they can bring to court. And it's even more astounding how much lying goes on in divorce cases. I once gave my investigative reporting students the assignment of digging into my background. One of them got into my parents' divorce file and made copies of some of the declarations. I read through my mother's descriptions of what my father was doing to us kids. Every so often I'd turn back to the front page to make sure I was reading the right file. A whole lot of it was pure fiction. She had portrayed the right man and spoke of events that really happened, but the facts were distorted. It reminded me of the U.S. government's descriptions of those massive battles our troops fought on the nation island of Grenada.

Keep that in mind when you read through a divorce file, a lot of it may be exaggerated. You'll want to believe it's all true, but you'll be safer if you believe only about half of it. What's amazing to me is the number of times the allegations refer to outright illegal things. Following the plane crash death of rock legend Ricky Nelson, authorities speculated that maybe some of the passengers aboard the ill-fated DC-3 had been using illegal drugs. CBS News hired me to look for any history of drug use on the part of Nelson. As it turns out, he and his divorcing wife were fighting over the custody of their twin sons at the time of Nelson's death. One claim his wife made was that Nelson was unfit to care for the boys. In a declaration filed in open court, she alleged that her husband frequently used cocaine in their house. She provided enough details to make a compelling case against her singer husband.

In another divorce file the wife of a prominent city official accused her husband of using drugs, abusing their daughter and other crimes. He countered by accusing her of being a drug user as well as a devil worshipper. The courts should publish a best seller list of court cases.

Keep your eyes open for a file titled Reciprocal Enforcement Support Law (sometimes abbreviated as RESL or just REL). This file exists when either mom or dad leave the county and one of them fails to pay court-ordered child or spousal support. Since local authorities can't run all over the country collecting monthly checks, they rely on a federal law that requires district attorneys to collect payments from fathers or mothers in one county who owe support payments to an ex-spouse now living in another county. Every county is supposed to reciprocate with every other county in enforcing the support laws—thus the name, Reciprocal Enforcement Support Law. If the lawyer you're checking out is involved in one of these cases, you'll find a fat file in both the affected counties. The file contains some of the most personal information about father, mother and children—where the parents live and work, how much money they make, what their expenses are, names and ages of the kids, cars they drive and much, much more. This comes in handy if you sue your attorney and need to prove he has assets.

Probate Court

Depending on the state you're in, probate court could be a function of the county superior court, the family law court, or could be a separate court of its own. Any clerk at any level of government should know where to find the probate records. Probate court exists to resolve disputes over who gets what when someone with assets dies.

Where there's a will, there's a family. And when there's a will, there's a fight—because where there's a will, there's someone who feels cheated. And when there's someone who feels cheated, there's a probate judge who will settle the dispute and make certain things are distributed fairly.

If there's a will, expect to find it in the case file at probate court. Wills are wonderful because they tell you how, ultimately, somebody really felt about their family members. Forget everything Grandpa told you he felt about you. The proof is in the will. Make it a point to check the probate files of the parents and grandparents of the person you're investigating.

Usually it reads something like this: "To my son Daniel I leave $25,000 and the ranch. To my son Robert I leave $25,000 and my Rolls Royce. To my daughter Barbara I leave $25,000 and the Miami Beach condominium. And to my so-called son Butch, the lawyer, I leave $1. And if he even so much as whines one time about it, he won't even get the damned dollar."

Now in the event the lawyer you're investigating was left a good sum of money, look for that brother or sister who Dad or Grandpa stiffed and give him or her a call. I promise they have been hating their sibling since the day the will was read. They'll tell you any dirt you want to know.

Within the probate case file you'll also find an accounting of where the money and property ultimately went. You'll also find a list of creditors who never got paid by the decedent before he died. Again, if you decide to sue your attorney, here's a great place to find assets he may have inherited. And the file may tell you the names and addresses of other family members, and some clues to geographical areas that might have other records relating to your attorney or his family.

Bankruptcy Court

Bankruptcy court is a function of the U.S. District court in your area. There may not be a federal court in your area, but there is certainly one within an hour or two of where you live. It's at this court that you'll find the files relating to civil and criminal cases filed in federal court. But there's almost always a bankruptcy court there, too.

Bankruptcy cases are so directly telling of the character of the attorney you're investigating that you absolutely must go take a peek into the file. First you're going to see some sob story as to how he got into a financial jam and how he can't possibly pay off all his debts and "Your honor, would you please tell them I don't have to pay them all back, please?"

Within the file you'll find the names and addresses of all the people he owes and the amount they say is due them. Then you'll find a listing of the assets that remained at the time the case was filed and how much each creditor would get. Usually, no one makes out except the person filing the bankruptcy.

Be sure to look through the indices for years preceding and following the bankruptcy you found. You're likely to find more of them. Some of these scoundrels will file for bankruptcy every few years. You need to know about this pattern if you're going to rely on an attorney to represent you. If he goes belly up in the middle of your case, who's to say you won't be one of the people grabbing and pushing to get a piece of whatever he didn't squander?

I spoke with a woman who was badly injured in a traffic accident. Even though her father and two of her brothers were attorneys, she took her case to a slick, big city attorney. Turns out he was collecting settlement money earmarked for her and using it to buy cocaine. He snorted her entire settlement. He even snorted some money her insurance company advanced her to get immediate medical attention. The terms of her policy said she was to reimburse the $10,000 after she collected the money from the other party in the accident. She didn't even know he had received the advance on her behalf. Then, she says, he staggered into court, high on something. The judge kicked him out of the court room and ruled in favor of the other party. The client received a total of $500 from the attorney. Then, a few years later, her insurance company sued her seeking the $10,000 they had advanced her attorney. He has since filed for bankruptcy, quit his practice and checked himself into a detox clinic. She was stuck with the $10,000 bill.

Naturalization Court

While you're at the bankruptcy court, ask them if there's also a naturalization court nearby. It's a function of the U.S. District Court. If your attorney was born in a foreign country and tried to become a U.S. citizen, he had to have petitioned the naturalization court. Part of the petition process involves filling out a lengthy questionnaire that probes into the applicant's life both in the old country and here in the United States. The applicant must list two or three people who know him to be of good character.

This is also one of the places where a person can legally change his name. If he just doesn't like his old name of Ivan Pafoofnicacheck, here's a chance for him to legally change it to a more American-sounding name—like maybe Steve Pafoofnicacheck. He could even change his last name if he wanted.

This is one of the rare government offices where you cannot copy the public record file. You'd better take a pad of paper. Oh, and be sure to look for multiple applications. Many people apply for citizenship, fill out the application and then fail to follow through in time. The system requires them to submit a new application. I've found as many as three applications for the same person. The funny thing was that one guy never listed the same character reference twice. Not only did I get the names of nine of his so-called friends, I was also able to speculate that he might have had trouble keeping friends for very long.

Tax Court

Your attorney's personal and corporate federal income tax files are not open to the public—that is, unless he goes to U.S. Tax Court. Since it's sort of a civil trial—a dispute between two parties (him and the government) in open court—his income tax returns and related documents become a matter of public record. This will give you one of the best glimpses of his financial position.

Most tax cases are heard at the tax court in Washington, DC. Call your nearest U.S. District Court to see if they may also be hearing tax cases.

Other Courts and Hearings

They vary by state, but there are many other places where someone may appear before a judge, an administrative law judge, a commission or some other judicial panel.

These might include the worker's compensation appeals board, the state or federal labor board, state or federal equal opportunity boards, the state bar court, consumer licensing boards and many more. It's a good idea to order a copy of your state's government phone directory from your state capital. It usually costs no more than $10–15, often much less. By leafing through it for a few minutes you'll find more bureaucratic nooks and crannies than you've ever imagined. You never know—your attorney may own a piece of a race horse and has been called before the horse racing board for some violation. The more you get to know about your attorney, the more places you'll find where you can look for dirt.

STATE RECORDS

Motor Vehicle and Driving Records

Many states allow open inspection of driving records and vehicle-registration files. In other states you may have to hire a private investigator who has legal access to the records.

You should be able to get certain information off your attorney's driver's license record. It should include his name, date of birth, address, the issue date, expiration date and any restrictions (glasses, can't drive at night, etc.). You should also be able to access, at the very least, his most recent driving record. Ask the clerk for information about any citations he's received, including the violation date, the conviction date, the court that heard the case, the section of the vehicle code he violated, the citation number, and the license number of the vehicle he was driving. Armed with this information you may be able to go to the court and view the complete citation. That will give you the name of the officer who cited him, information about where he was and which direction he was going, how many other people were in the car with him and much more.

You may also be able to find out if he failed to appear in court following any citation or if he was arrested for driving under the influence.

And many states still allow you to determine which vehicles are registered to a particular person. Usually you need to know the correct name of the person and a valid address. You'll get back the license number of the vehicle, the name and address of the legal owner (usually a bank or credit union if the car isn't paid off), the make, body style, date first registered and the Vehicle Identification Number (VIN). Sometimes you can also ask if there are any parking tickets attached to the vehicle.

It's also possible in some states to buy a vehicle history report. This is a complete record of everyone who's owned the vehicle over the years.

Don't forget when you're checking with the motor vehicle department to ask about motorcycles, boats, trailers or any other types of vehicles they may register. And, of course, if you already know the license number of a vehicle, the motor vehicle department should be able to tell you the name and address of the registered owner and the legal owner.

Secretary of State

The secretary of state is like a county clerk, but on a much larger scale. This office will keep track of corporations operating in the state, partnerships, limited partnerships, limited liability companies, notaries, Uniform Commercial Code filings and statewide campaign contributions. Depending on your state, it could be just one office or a separate office for each of the functions listed above.

Corporations

If a corporation does business in your state, it probably has to register with the secretary of state. Just call directory assistance in your state capital to get the phone number. Most secretary of state offices will give you information over the phone. Others charge a fee or are available on commercial databases.

The staff should be able to provide you with the name of the corporation, any prior name for it, the main address, the corporation number, the state of incorporation, the current status and, if the corporation is incorporated in your state, the names of the various officers (president/CEO, vice president, secretary, treasurer and agent for service of process—often an attorney), their addresses, the original articles of incorporation and any amendments or name changes.

If the corporation was incorporated in another state, you can usually call that state's secretary of state and get most of the same information over the phone.

Partnerships and Limited Partnerships

Your secretary of state may also keep track of partnerships and limited partnerships. A partnership is, as the name implies, a coalition of two or more individuals or legal entities (general partners). Since their money gets mixed up together and since they often use a made-up name, the secretary of state likes to get involved. You should be able to learn the names and addresses of all the general partners as well as the date the partnership was first registered with the state.

A limited partnership is a bit different. In a limited partnership there's at least one general partner as well as one or more (usually several) limited partners. The general partner gets to make the day-to-day decisions about how the company is run. He is also the one who accepts all the liabilities and risks that come with running a company. The limited partners are more akin to silent partners. They aren't allowed to get their fingers in the day-to-day running of the company and they can't easily be sued for the actions of the company.

Many times the limited partnership exists as a way for investors to team up to buy real estate. Unfortunately, in many states you aren't allowed to learn the names of the limited partners. If that's the case in your state, check with the county clerk in the county where the company is located. It's possible they had to file a fictitious name statement or an assumed name statement. And there's a good chance you may find the limited partners signing powers of attorney which allow someone else to sign deeds or other papers on their behalf. You'd find that at the recorder's office. Be sure to check the recorder's office in any county in any state where the limited partnership might own property.

There's a fairly new animal out there in the partnership business called a limited liability company or LLC. It's sort of a hybrid—a cross between a corporation and a limited partnership. It allows the benefits of being part of a corporation while still allowing some of the protection provided by a limited partnership. The papers should be open for inspection. Also, some states allow a similar type entity called a family limited liability company. This is designed to help families avoid many of the taxes involved when the patriarch passes away. Instead of Dad being the sole owner of his assets or the family business, the family limited liability company allows the young son or daughter to be the family business's legal owner before Pop passes on.

Notary Public Information

Remember, the recorder will not record a document unless one or both of the parties signs it. And unless the recorder personally witnesses the person signing it (almost never), a state-commissioned notary public must witness the signing after checking the identification of the person signing. Many states require the notary to keep a log of every signature he notarizes. The log may include identifying information about the person signing.

If you can't locate the notary at the office of the recorder or city/county clerk, look for a listing at the secretary of state's office. Some states will only verify that the notary is, indeed, commissioned to work in their state.

Uniform Commercial Code

The Uniform Commercial Code (UCC) is a set of laws each state subscribes to which makes doing business consistent in every state. However, to many people, the term Uniform Commercial Code refers to one part of the code—the part that protects people who loan money to people or businesses.

Lenders often want some sort of collateral before they loan money. Frequently, the collateral is a piece of equipment—a computer system, a piece of machinery, a valuable possession or any physical asset except real estate and vehicles.

The law requires anyone using a piece of personal property or equipment as collateral to publicly declare to the world that the particular item has already been spoken for. This prevents three or four lenders discovering they all loaned money to some turkey using the same piece of equipment as collateral.

The UCC filings have become a great way of identifying both people and their assets. Usually the UCC entry will show a Social Security number or a Federal Tax Identification number. Either of these numbers can be the key to discovering other information about the attorney you're investigating.

Keep in mind that many of the files kept at the office of the secretary of state are available on commercial databases such as Nexis or on CD-ROM. I suggest you make a call to the secretary of state and ask which vendors handle or resell their records to the public.

Campaign Contributions

The secretary of state also keeps track of campaign contributions relating to statewide elections and ballot measures. You may be able to review contributions by looking up the name of the candidate or ballot measure. Also, some states keep track of how much money each contributor gives. This means you can run the name of your attorney and see who he supports. See Appendix A for Internet access.

Consumer Affairs Regulators

Most states also license professionals such as contractors, hair dressers, doctors, psychologists, private investigators, automobile repair persons, accountants, electricians, funeral directors, etc.

You should be able to call the agency directly and verify if your attorney might also be licensed to do plumbing or repossessing or to cut your hair. Usually the information they can give you is limited to the date he became licensed, his work address, date of birth and, in some cases, the schools he attended. Of course, if there are any major complaints or actions against the professional, the consumer board or agency may provide you with the information.

FEDERAL RECORDS

U.S. Postal Service

There was a time when you could walk into any post office, slap down a dollar and get anyone's recent forwarding address. But that's now gone the route of a ten-cent cup of coffee. However, what you can still do to find a newer address for someone is to send a letter to the old address with the words "Do Not Forward—Address Correction Requested" emblazoned in big letters somewhere on the front of the envelope. As the message instructs, they won't forward it. Instead, they'll return it to you with the new forwarding address.

The only problem is that maybe the person didn't move, or the postal clerk will miss the message and the lawyer you're investigating will receive the envelope. What do you put in it? A private investigator friend of mine came up with a clever way of preventing the person he's investigating from finding out who sent the letter. He goes to a nearby restaurant or retail store that has a display of credit card applications. He puts the application in the envelope and puts a post office box return address with no name. Hopefully, if the person gets the mail, he'll either chuck it into the waste paper basket or apply for the credit card—never making note of the return address.

You still have the right to certain information on a person or firm's post office box application—that is, if you can prove to the postal clerk that the box holder is using the box for business purposes. Simply show the clerk an ad, a business card, stationery or an invoice showing the box to be involved in a business and you should be able to learn the true name of the box holder and his true delivery address. If you're really lucky or clever, you might end up actually looking at the entire application. If you get even brief access to it, jot down the person's phone number and driver's license number. This could help you further down the line.

Federal Election Commission

It's possible the attorney you're checking out is patriotic or politically inclined enough to want to help out a candidate or ballot measure by contributing money. If he contributes to a campaign at the federal level, you can check out how much he gave and to whom. The folks at the FEC will make copies from paper for 5¢ per page or from microfilm for only 15¢ per page. You just need to call them (800/424-9530) and tell the name of the contributor. You can also ask them about how you can use your computer and modem to dial into their computer using a prepaid account. See Appendix A for Internet access.

Federal Aviation Administration

A lot of attorneys are rich or important enough to own an airplane or at least have a pilot's license. For the cost of a phone call to Oklahoma you can check it out. If he's a pilot, the FAA folks will release his complete name, address, rating (what kind of aircraft he's qualified to fly), the date of his last medical exam and his license number. You can also give the FAA the attorney's name and they'll tell you if he owns an aircraft. If you identify the aircraft this way—or if you already know the wing number—they'll tell you all about the plane. You'll learn its type, the number people it seats, the number of engines, when it was manufactured, when it was bought, and much more. You can call them at (405) 954-3261. If you want to find out about his medical certification, call (405) 954-4821. And if he has had any accidents or violations, you can learn all about them by calling (405) 954-4173. If the phone call is too much for you, send them a note at the address listed in Apendix C. For rush orders, you can send them a blank check by overnight mail marked "Not to exceed $10." They'll send you either hard copies or microfiche. Also see Appendix A for Internet access.

Securities and Exchange Commission

When corporations offer stock for sale to the general public, Uncle Sam requires them to file various reports with the Securities and Exchange Commission. And if your lawyer is involved with the corporation as either an officer, agent or major stockholder, you're likely to find information about him in one of the many files. The agency turns over much of its public record files to a company called Disclosure Inc. This service will provide you with copies of the various reports that may include reference to the attorney's position, holdings, salary, benefits or other perks. To locate the Disclosure Inc. office nearest you, call the Los Angeles office at (800) 843-7747 or the Bethesda, MD office at (800) 638-8241.

National Personnel Records Center

If your attorney was ever in the U.S. military, you're likely to find information about him at the National Personnel Records Center. It's the starting point to find information about a former member of the military. You can either use a Standard Form 180 (Request for Military Information) or submit a typed letter in the form of a Freedom of Information Act (FOIA) request. You pretty much need to know the person's name, age or date of birth, branch of service and, preferably, the date of entrance and/or discharge.

There is no fee charged for FOIA requests from NPRC. However, responses can take 3–4 months. In your FOIA request you should ask for all releasable information. They will provide the following:

- Marital status
- Dependents (name, sex, age)
- Rank or grade and date of salary
- Present and past duty assignments
- Future assignments
- Office phone numbers
- Source of commission
- Military and civilian education level
- Promotion sequence number
- Decorations and/or awards
- Education and schooling
- Duty status
- Photograph
- Records of court martial trials (unclassified)
- Serial number or service number
- Hometown
- Date of birth

They will not provide Social Security number, home address or other personal information.

For those seriously interested in finding anyone who was in the military get *How to Locate Anyone Who Is or Has Been in the Military* by Richard S. Johnson, (800) 937-2133.

Chapter Six

☑ *How to Use the Information*

Now that you've learned practically everything you could imagine about the attorney, what will you do with the information? If you've uncovered anything that would make you feel uncomfortable working with him, it might be a good idea to switch attorneys. You don't need to tell the attorney why you want to terminate his services. You could tell him the arrangement just doesn't feel right. That should do it.

There's no reason for letting him know you dug into his personal life if you're not planning to work with him. If there is just one thing that's bothering you about him, consider asking some vague questions to see if he responds honestly.

For example, he may have been suspended from the bar in the past or may be on probation now. It's not improper to ask him if he has had any disciplinary actions taken against him by the state bar. If he says he hasn't, you should probably realize you're dealing with someone who doesn't want to be honest with you. Even then, there may be no benefit to confronting him with his lies unless you're not sure you checked out the right attorney and you feel a need for some clarification.

If you've found information about his personal life that bothers you—perhaps he regularly beats his wife—you'll have to consider whether that affects how he'll function as an attorney in your case. Personally, I'd never tolerate the use of drugs or any indication of violent behavior. Of course, to the drug user or wife beater these things may not be too big a deal.

A rule of thumb, however, is that almost no one reacts nicely when they learn you've been poking around into their personal or professional lives. You may want to tell someone about the groovy things you've uncovered. May I suggest you bite your tongue. Even telling your friends could backfire on you. An angry attorney could claim you were trying to defame him. It would be a tough case to prove if you stuck to the public records, but when you're yanked into court—especially by an attorney—you've already lost.

If you've investigated an attorney because he represents your opponent in a lawsuit, you'll probably want to consult your own attorney to see how, or if, the information you came up with could help your case. I hope you checked out your own attorney first.

Appendix A

☑ *Internet Resources*

Consumer Awareness and Safety

http://www.islandnet.com/~wwlia/police.htm
Safety tips and ways to handle certain matters such as annoying phone calls, etc. Includes links to other sites.

http://police.sas.ab.ca
Copnet: law enforcement sites.

http://lmc.einet.net:8000/galaxy/Community.html
Consumer and community issues.

http://www.member.com/aca/pub25g.html
Solve It: a debt collection web site for consumers, collectors, credit grantors and media.

http://www.abanet.org/publiced/consumers.html
Books, booklets and brochures published by ABA for the general public.

http://www.barlinc.org
NC Bar Association homepage with numerous links.

http://www.barlinc.org/livwill.html
Discusses various aspects of the living will and includes actual living will forms.

http://seamless.com/talf/txt/complain.html
Discusses several strategies for resolving consumer complaints, including filing suit.

http://seamless.com/talf/txt/article/legalfee.shtml
Discusses hourly fees, contingency fees, etc. Things a consumer should know before signing an agreement with a lawyer.

http://seamless.com/talf/txt/article/howhire.shtm
Tips on hiring a lawyer, including mistakes to avoid and questions to ask.

http://consumerlawpage.com
The Consumer Law Page (winner of Magellan 3-Star Award): contains articles of various topics of interest to consumers, a list of 100 consumer information brochures and 1000+ Internet resources.

gopher://gopher.gsa.gov/00/cic/money/ccredit
Discusses Consumer Credit Protection Act of 1968, which protects the rights of single women, the elderly and all who use credit.

Court Records

http://www.uscourts.gov/PubAccess.html
Directory of Electronic Public Access to Court Records. Various public access services to federal court information are listed. For many records, the user must pre-register by calling a given phone number and paying a user access fee of 60¢ per minute. Included are U.S. Supreme Court, U.S. Circuit Courts of Appeal, District and Bankruptcy Courts.

Education

http://www.ilrg.com/cle_ref.html
Site for attorneys and paralegals which includes state requirements for continuing education and various places which offer courses.

http://www.law.cornell.edu
Offers recent and historic Supreme Court decisions, e-mail address directory of faculty and staff at U.S. law schools, and various legal information.

http://www.law.indiana.edu:80/law/v-lib/orgs.html
The World Wide Web Virtual Library of Law Organizations: includes a search area.

http://www.abanet.org/publiced/home.html
Site of ABA Division for Public Education.

http://www.abanet.org/publiced/journalists.html
Site of ABA Division of Public Education for journalists

Family Law Issues

http://www.islandnet.com/~wwlia/us-uifsa.htm
Information on child support with links to state legal information centers and other topics.

http://www.islandnet.com/~wwlia/us-cus.htm
Information on child custody with links to U.S. Law Office and Legal Information Center.

http://www.nolo.com/briefs.hhtml
Nolo's Reference Library: Reference encyclopedia concerning various topics including small business, employment rights, wills, consumer issues, tax problems and many others. Many links are provided.

Humor

http://www.nolo.com/jokes/jokes.html
Lawyer jokes.

Insurance

http://seamless.com/commons/html#insurance-law
Insurance Consumers Survival Guide and Lawyer's Insurance Resources page.

Newsgroups

http://www.kentlaw.edu/lawnet/llawnet.html
Legal profession mailing lists and discussion groups with searchable index.

http://www.law.cornell.edu/listservs
Archives of listserv sites.

Law Links

http://www.kentlaw.edu/lawlinks/index.html
Law-oriented indexes on web and links to law schools and
law libraries.

http://www.wakefieldpd.org/courts.html
Many legal sites, including Virtual Law Library, Attorney
Net and others.

http://www.kybar.org/legal.htm
Links to Kentucky legal sites, U.S. Federal Statutes, U.S.
Government Resources, state bar associations, attorney lists,
and business sites. Includes directories and search engines.

http://www.bpd.org/courts.htm
Courts, law and legal sites.

http://www.ironclad.com/gen-ref.html
MacMillan Lytle Fisher's site of legal reference sites, includ-
ing the topics: American, Canadian and General Collections,
Virtual Law Libraries, Finding Lawyers, Law Journals and
Newsletters Online.

http://lcweb.loc.gov/homepage/online.html#z3950
Site for searching the Library of Congress catalogs.

http://www.lawsource.com/also
Compilation of links to on-line sources of American law
that are available without charge (includes U.S., Canada and
Mexico).

http://www.laws.com/attorneys.html
Lawyers and law firms on the web.

http://www.law.upenn.edu/library/misc.html
Miscellaneous legal sites (over 100 sites).

http://www.sw.com/gen_info/legal.html
Schopf & Weiss Legal Sites Page: Legal sites, directory of
law firms, legal directory and expert witness database.

http://www.abanet.org/lawlink/home.html
  ABA links to other legal research and information sources.

Media/News

http://www.islandnet.com/~wwlia/news.htm
  World Wide Legal News Magazine published by World
Wide Legal Information Association.

http://www.courttv.com
  Court TV Law Center contains casefiles, legal help and
various law links.

Patent and Copyright

http://town.hall.org/patent/patent/html
  Access to 26 years of U.S. Patent and Trademark Office
patent descriptions (images of patents are available from the
last 17 years).

http://www.ljx.com/copyright
  Copyright statutes and resources.

Religion

http://www.clsnet.com/welcome.html
  Christian Legal Society web site.

Miscellaneous Resources

http://www.ilrg.com/non-profit.html
  Non-profit associations, organizations and services.

http://www.islandnet.com/~wwlia/wwlia.htm
  WWLIA (World Wide Legal Information Assn) miscellaneous legal sites.

http://www.islandnet.com/~wwlia/diction.htm
  WWLIA legal dictionary.

http://www.islandnet.com/~wwlia/us-dir.htm
  WWLIA directory of U.S. legal organizations.

http://www.islandnet.com/~wwlia/us-home.htm
WWLIA link to U.S. Legal Information Center, including many legal links.

http://www.islandnet.com/~wwlia/webusca.htm
WWLIA directory of California attorneys and law firm home pages.

http://www.islandnet.com/~wwlia/us-whos.htm
WWLIA miscellaneous legal sites.

http://www.laws.com/legal_resource.html
Law resources, including attorney search, organizations and many other links.

http://www.ljextra.com/practice/corporate/index.html
Resources available for corporate law.

http://www.ilrg.com
Internet Legal Resources Guide: a catagorized index of 3100 web sites concerning law and the legal profession. Included is the Legal Forms Archive.

http://www.ilrg.com/ref_resources.html
ILRG's References and Resources Menu.

http://www.lawcrawler.com
Find Law: a search site for law-related items, plus numerous links to other sites.

http://www.westpub.com/htbin/htimage/cahom.conf?60,186
Computer-assisted legal research.

http://www.wld.com
West's legal directory and search site for lawyers and law offices in U.S. and Canada.

http://www.martindale.com/
Martindale's directory and search site.

http://www.barlinc.org
North Carolina Bar Association page with many links.

http://www.attorney.com
AttorneyNet home page containing a search for attorneys and other legal links.

http://www.attorney.com/lawlinks.html
AttorneyNet site containing various legal links, including commercial codes, tax codes, U.S. Supreme Court decisions.

http://hg.org/wrtopic.html
Hieros Gamos: Comprehensive Legal Site of the World, with over 15,000 original pages and more than 30,000 links.

http://www.hg.org/1351.txt
Gives definition of "handicap" and what constitutes "reasonable accommodation."

http://law.uark.edu/arklaw/legallist.txt
Legal List: a site of law-related resources on the Internet and elsewhere.

http://www.tray.com/fecinfo/
Federal Election Commission records showing all political contributors of over $200.

http://www.amcity.com
American City Business Journals. See if your lawyer has been written up in the local business press.

http://www.infophil.com/World/Alumni/
World Alumni Net. Searchable by college, last name and year of graduation.

http://chamber-of-commerce.com/coc/chamber.htm
Contact information for chambers of commerce worldwide.

http://www.nysed.gov/prof/profhome.htm
Online license verification and summaries of professional discipline cases for New York state only.

http://www.via net/test.html
FAA aircraft registration database. This information is about 4 years old.

http:http://www.bop.gov/
Federal Bureau of Prisons gives you a complete nationwide
listing of prisons and their stats and phone numbers (just in case
your person is "tied up" at the moment).

http://www.abii.com/
  Look-up USA. Search for businesses or people by name
with American Directory Assistance or search by type of
business with American Yellow Pages.

http://www.familytreemaker.com/00000229.html
  Gives county court house addresses.

http://local.yahoo.com/bin/get_local
  City to county locator criss-cross. Find the county when
you know only the city.

Appendix B

✓ *State Government Sources*

ALABAMA

State government information number: (334) 242-8000

Department of Public Safety
Driver License Division
PO Box 1471
Montgomery, AL 36102-1471
(334) 242-4400

Alabama State Bar
415 Dexter Avenue
Montgomery, AL 36104
(334) 269-1515, (334) 261-6310 Fax
http://www.alabar.com

Secretary of State
Corporation Section
PO Box 5616
Montgomery, AL 36103-5616
(334) 242-5324 (Corporations)
(334) 242-5325 (Trade Names)
(334) 240-3138 Fax

U.S. Bankruptcy Court
Middle District of Alabama
Montgomery Division
PO Box 1248
Montgomery, AL 36102-1248
(334) 223-7250

U.S. Bankruptcy Court
Northern District of Alabama
Robert S. Vance Federal Building
1800 5th Ave, N, Room 120
Birmingham, AL 35203
(205) 731-0850

U.S. Bankrupcty Court
Northern District of Alabama
PO Box 1289
Decatur, AL 35602
(205) 353-2817

U.S. Bankruptcy Court
Northern District of Alabama
Western Division
PO Box 3226
Tuscaloosa, AL 35403
(205) 752-0426

U.S. Bankruptcy Court
Southern District of Alabama
PO Box 2865
Mobile, AL 36652
(334) 441-5391

ALASKA
State government information number: (907) 465-2111

Department of Public Safety
Driver Services, Driving Records
PO Box 20020
Juneau, AK 99802-0020
(907) 465-4335, (907) 463-5860 Fax

Alaska Bar Association
510 "L" Street, #602
Anchorage, AK 99501
(907) 272-7469, (907) 272-2932 Fax
E-mail: alaskabar@alaskabar.org

Department of Commerce
Corporation Section
PO Box 11080
Juneau, AK 99811
(907) 465-2530

U.S. Bankruptcy Court
605 W. 4th Avenue, Suite 138
Anchorage, AK 99501-2296
(907) 271-2655

ARIZONA
State government information number: (602) 542-4900

Department of Transportation
Room 504M
1801 W. Jefferson
Phoenix, AZ 85007
(602) 255-8357

State Bar of Arizona
111 W. Monroe Street, Suite 1800
Phoenix, AZ 85003-1742
(602) 252-4804
(602) 271-4930 Fax
E-mail: azbar@azbar.org

Arizona Corporation Commission
PO Box 6019
Phoenix, AZ 85005
(602) 542-3026

Bankruptcy Records
U.S. Bankruptcy Court
PO Box 34151
Phoenix, AZ 85067-4151
(602) 640-5800

U.S. Bankruptcy Court
110 S. Church Ave, Rm 8112
Tuscon, AZ 85701-1608
(520) 620-7500

U.S. Bankruptcy Court
325 W. 19th Street, Suite D
Yuma, AZ 85364
(520) 783-2288

ARKANSAS
State government information number: (501) 682-3000

Traffic Violation Records, Room 123
PO Box 1272
Little Rock, AR 72203
(800) 662-8247

Arkansas Bar Association
400 West Markham
Little Rock, AR 72201
(501) 375-4606, (501) 375-4901 Fax
http://www.arbar.com

Secretary of State
Corporation Division
State Capitol Bldg, Room 058
Little Rock, AR 72201-1094
(501) 682-5151

U.S. Bankruptcy Court
Eastern District of Arkansas
U.S. Courthouse
600 W. Capitol Avenue, Suite 101
Little Rock, AR 72201-3325
(501) 324-6357

U.S. Bankruptcy Court
Western District of Arkansas
PO Box 3097
Fayetteville, AR 72702-3097
(501) 582-9800

CALIFORNIA
State government information numbers:
        (916) 322-9900, (213) 897-9900

Department of Motor Vehicles
Bond and Control Department
PO Box 944231
Sacramento, CA 94244-2310
(916) 657-6557

State Bar of CA (North)
455 Franklin Street
San Francisco, CA 94102
(415) 561-8200, (415) 561-8228 Fax
http://www.calbar.org

State Bar of CA (South)
1149 S. Hill St, 4th Flr
Los Angeles, CA 90015
(213) 765-1000
State hotline: (800) 843-9053

Secretary of State
1230 "J" Street
Sacramento, CA 95814
(916) 445-0620

U.S. Bankruptcy Court
Central District of California
Roybal Federal Building and Courthouse
255 East Temple St, Room 1260
Los Angeles, CA 90012-4754
(213) 894-6046

U.S. Bankruptcy Court
Central District of California
516 Federal Building
34 Civic Center Plaza
Santa Ana, CA 92701
(714) 836-2993

U.S. Bankruptcy Court Clerk
Central District of California
105 Federal Building
699 North Arrowhead Avenue
San Bernardino, CA 92401
(909) 383-5742

U.S. Bankruptcy Court Clerk
Central District of California
Northern Division
222 E. Carrillo
Santa Barbara, CA 93101
(805) 897-3880

U.S. Bankruptcy Court
Eastern District of California
650 Capitol Mall
8308 U.S. Courthouse
Sacramento, CA 95814
(916) 498-5525

U.S. Bankruptcy Court
Eastern District of California
1130 "O" Street
2656 U.S. Courthouse
Fresno, CA 93721
(209) 498-7217

U.S. Bankruptcy Court
Eastern District of California
PO Box 5276
Modesto, CA 95352
(209) 521-5160

U.S. Bankruptcy Court
Northern District of California
PO Box 7341
San Francisco, CA 94120-7341
(415) 705-3200

U.S. Bankruptcy Court
Northern District of California
U.S. Courthouse, Room 3035
280 South First Street
San Jose, CA 95113-3099
(408) 535-5118

U.S. Bankruptcy Court
Northern District of California
PO Box 2070
Oakland, CA 94604
(510) 273-7212

U.S. Bankruptcy Court
Northern District of California
99 South "E" Street
Santa Rosa, CA 95404
(707) 525-8520

U.S. Bankruptcy Court
Southern District of California
Jacob Weinberger U.S. Courthouse
325 West F Street
San Diego, CA 92101-6017
(619) 557-5620

COLORADO
State government information number: (303) 866-5000

Motor Vehicle Division
Traffic Records
140 W. 6th Avenue
Denver, CO 80204
(303) 572-56113

Colorado Bar Association
1900 Grant, #950
Denver, CO 80203
(303) 860-1115
(303) 894-0821 Fax
http://www.usa.net/cobar/index.htm

Secretary of State
Corporation Division
1560 Broadway, Suite 200
Denver, CO 80202
(303) 894-2251, (900) 555-1515 Fax

U.S. Bankruptcy Court
District of Colorado
U.S. Custom House
721 19th Street
Denver, CO 80202-2508
(303) 844-4045

CONNECTICUT
State government information number: (203) 566-2211

Department of Motor Vehicles
Copy Records Unit
60 State Street
Weathersfield, CT 06109
(203) 566-2240

Connecticut Bar Association
101 Corporate Place
Rocky Hill, CT 06067-1894
(860) 721-0025, (860) 257-4125 Fax
http://www.ctbar.org

Secretary of State
Corporation Division
30 Trinity Street
Hartford, CT 06106
(203) 566-8570

U.S. Bankruptcy Court
District of Connecticut
Federal Building and U.S. Courthouse
450 Main Street
Hartford, CT 06103
(203) 240-3675

U.S. Bankruptcy Court
District of Connecticut
Federal Building and U.S. Courthouse
915 Lafayette Boulevard
Bridgeport, CT 06604
(203) 579-5808

DELAWARE
State government information number: (800) 273-9500

Division of Motor Vehicles
Route 113, Bay Road
PO Box 698
Dover, DE 19903
(302) 739-4497

Delaware State Bar Association
1201 Orange Street, #1100
Wilmington, DE 19801
(302) 658-5279, (302) 658-5212 Fax

Secretary of State
Department of Corporation
PO Box 898
Dover, DE 19903
(302) 739-3073
U.S. Bankruptcy Court
District of Delaware
Marine Midland Plaza
824 Market Street
Wilmington, DE 19801
(302) 573-6174

DISTRICT OF COLUMBIA
District government operator: (202) 727-1000

Bureau of Motor Vehicles
Driving Records
301 "C" Street, N.W., Room 1157
Washington, DC 20001
(202) 727-6761

District of Columbia Bar
1250 "H" Street, N.W., 6th Floor
Washington, DC 20005
(202) 737-4700, (202) 626-3472 Fax
http://www.dcbar.org

Bar Association of the District of Columbia
1819 "H" Street, N.W., 12th Floor
Washington, DC 20006-3690
(202) 223-6600, (202) 293-3388 Fax
E-mail: barassn@aol.com

Department of Consumer and Regulatory Affairs
614 H Street, N.W.
Room 407
Washington, DC 20001
(202) 727-7278

U.S. Bankruptcy Court
U.S. Courthouse
333 Constitution Avenue, N.W.
Washington, DC 20001-2866
(202) 273-0042

FLORIDA
State government information number: (904) 488-1234

Dept of Highway Safety & Motor Vehicles
ATTN: Records Department
2900 Apalache Parkway
Tallahassee, FL 32309-0575
(904) 487-2370

The Florida Bar
650 Apalachee Parkway
Tallahassee, FL 32399-2300
(904) 561-5600, (904) 561-5827 Fax
http://www.flabar.org

Department of State
Division of Corporations
Certification Section
PO Box 6327
Tallahssee, FL 32314
(904) 487-6053

U.S. Bankruptcy Court
Middle District of Florida
4921 Memorial Hwy, Ste 205
Tampa, FL 33634
(813) 243-5162

U.S. Bankruptcy Court
Middle District of Florida
PO Box 559
Jacksonville, FL 32201-0559
(904) 232-2852

U.S. Bankruptcy Court
Middle District of Florida
135 W. Central Blvd, Ste 950
Orlando, FL 32801
(407) 648-6364

U.S. Bankruptcy Court
Northern District of Florida
227 N. Bronough St, Room 3120
Tallahassee, FL 32301
(904) 942-8933

U.S. Bankruptcy Court
Northern District of Florida
220 West Garden Street, Ste 700
Pensacola, FL 32501
(904) 435-8475

U.S. Bankruptcy Court
Southern District of Florida
1401 Federal Building
51 S.W. First Avenue
Miami, FL 33130
(305) 536-5216

GEORGIA

State government information number: (404) 656-2000
Department of Public Safety
Driver Services
PO Box 1456
Atlanta, GA 30371
(404) 624-7487

State Bar of Georgia
800 Hurt Building
50 Hurt Plaza
Atlanta, GA 30303
(404) 527-8700
(404) 527-8717 Fax
http://gabar.org

Secretary of State
Corporation Division
2 Martin Luther King, Jr. Drive
315 W. Tower
Atlanta, GA 30334
(404) 656-2817

U.S. Bankruptcy Court
Middle District of Georgia
PO Box 1957
Macon, GA 31202
(912) 752-3506

U.S. Bankruptcy Court
Middle District of Georgia
PO Box 2147
Columbus, GA 31902
(706) 649-7837

U.S. Bankruptcy Court
Northern District of Georgia
Russell Federal Building and U.S. Courthouse
75 Spring St, SW, Room 1340
Atlanta, GA 30303-3367
(404) 215-1000

U.S. Bankruptcy Court
Northern District of Georgia
Federal Bldg, Room 203C
126 Washington Street, SW
Gainesville, GA 30501
(770) 536-0556

U.S. Bankruptcy Court
Northern District of Georgia
PO Box 2328
Newnan, GA 30264
(770) 251-5583

U.S. Bankruptcy Court
Northern District of Georgia
PO Box 5231
Rome, GA 30161
(706) 291-5639

U.S. Bankruptcy Court
Southern District of Georgia
PO Box 8347
Savannah, GA 31412
(912) 652-4100

U.S. Bankruptcy Court
Southern District of Georgia
PO Box 1487
Augusta, GA 30903
(706) 724-2421

HAWAII
State government information number: (808) 586-2211

District Court of First Circuit
Violations Bureau
ATTN: Abstract Department
1111 Alakea Street
Honolulu, HI 96813
(808) 548-5735

Hawaii State Bar Association
1136 Union Mall, Penthouse 1
Honolulu, HI 96813
(808) 537-1868, (808) 521-7936 Fax
E-mail: sjurich@hsba.org

Department of Commerce and Consumer Affairs
Business Registration Division
PO Box 40
Honolulu, HI 96810
(808) 586-2727

U.S. Bankruptcy Court
First Hawaiian Tower
1132 Bishop Street, Suite 250L
Honolulu, HI 96813
(808) 522-8100

IDAHO
State government information number: (208) 334-2411

Idaho Transportation Division
Driver Services
PO Box 34
Boise, ID 83731
(208) 334-8739

Idaho State Bar
525 W. Jefferson Street
Boise, ID 83701
(208) 334-4500, (208) 334-4515 Fax

Secretary of State
Corporations Division
PO Box 83720
Boise, ID 83720-0080
(208) 334-2300

U.S. Bankruptcy Court
District of Idaho
550 West Fort Street
U.S. Courthouse, MSC 042
Boise, ID 83724
(208) 334-9571

ILLINOIS
State government information number: (217) 782-2000

Motor Vehicle Services
2701 S. Kirksen Parkway
Springfield, IL 62723
(217) 782-2720

Illinois State Bar Association
424 South Second Street
Springfield, IL 62701
(217) 525-1760
(217) 525-0712 Fax
http://illinoisbar.org

Office of Secretary of State
Securities Department
900 S. Spring Street
Springfield, IL 62704
(217) 785-4929

U.S. Bankruptcy Court
PO Box 2438
Springfield, IL 62705-2438
(217) 492-4551

U.S. Bankruptcy Court
PO Box 657
Danville, IL 61834
(217) 431-4820

U.S. Bankruptcy Court
100 NE Monroe St
156 Federal Bldg
Peoria, IL 61202
(309) 671-7035

U.S. Bankruptcy Court
Everett Dirksen Building
219 S. Dearborne St, Room 710
Chicago, IL 60604
(312) 435-5587

U.S. Bankruptcy Court
Federal Building
211 S. Court Street
Rockford, IL 61101
(815) 987-4350

U.S. Bankruptcy Court
PO Box 309
East St. Louis, IL 62202
(618) 482-9400

U.S. Bankruptcy Court
U.S. Courthouse
301 W. Main Street
Benton, IL 62812
(618) 435-2200

INDIANA
State government information number: (317) 232-1000

Indiana Bureau of Motor Vehicles
Driver Records
Indiana Government Center N
100 N. Senate Avenue, Room N405
Indianapolis, IN 46204
(317) 232-2894

Indiana State Bar Association
230 E. Ohio Street, 4th Floor
Indianapolis, IN 46204
(317) 639-5465
(317) 266-2588 Fax
http://www.iquest.net/isba/

Secretary of State
302 W. Washington Street
Room EE018
Indianapolis, IN 46204
(317) 232-6576

U.S. Bankruptcy Court
Northern District of Indiana
Grant Federal Building and U.S. Courthouse
204 South Main St, Room 224
South Bend, IN 46601-2196
(219) 236-8247

U.S. Bankruptcy Court
Northern District of Indiana
1188 Federal Building
1300 S. Harrison Street
Ft. Wayne, IN 46802
(219) 420-5100

U.S. Bankruptcy Court
Northern District of Indiana
221 Federal Bldg
610 Connecticut Street
Gary, IN 46402
(219) 881-3335

U.S. Bankruptcy Court
Southern District of Indiana
U.S. Courthouse
46 E. Ohio Street
Indianapolis, IN 46204
(317) 226-6710

U.S. Bankruptcy Court
Southern District of Indiana
101 N.W. Martin Luther King Blvd
356 Federal Building
Evansville, IN 47708
(812) 465-6440

U.S. Bankruptcy Court
Southern District of Indiana
121 W. Spring St, 102 Federal Bldg
New Albany, IN 47150
(812) 948-5254

U.S. Bankruptcy Court
Southern District of Indiana
30 North 7th St, 203 Federal Bldg
Terre Haute, IN 47808
(812) 238-1550

IOWA
State government information number: (515) 281-5011

Department of Transportation
Office of Driver Services
PO Box 9204
Des Moines, IA 50306-9204
(515) 237-3070

Iowa State Bar Association
521 East Locust, 3rd Floor
Des Moines, IA 50309-1939
(515) 243-3179, (515) 243-2511 Fax
http://www.commonlink.com/isba

Secretary of State
Hoover Office Bldg
Des Moines, IA 50319
(515) 281-5204
(515) 242-5953 Fax

U.S. Bankruptcy Court
Northern District of Iowa
PO Box 74890
Cedar Rapids, IA 52407
(319) 362-9696

U.S. Bankruptcy Court
Northern District of Iowa
117 U.S. Courthouse
Sioux City, IA 51101
(712) 252-3757

U.S. Bankruptcy Court
PO Box 9264
Des Moines, IA 50306-9264
(515) 284-6230

KANSAS
State government information number: (913) 296-0111

Kansas Department of Revenue
Driver Control Bureau
Division of Vehicles
PO Box 12021
Topeka, KS 66616-2021
(913) 296-3671

Kansas Bar Association
1200 Harrison Street
Topeka, KS 66601
(913) 234-5696
(913) 234-3813 Fax
E-mail: ksbar@ink.org/public

Secretary of State
State Capitol, 2nd Floor
Topeka, KS 66612
(913) 296-4564
(913) 296-4570 Fax

U.S. Bankruptcy Court
District of Kansas
401 N. Market Street
167 U.S. Courthouse
Wichita, KS 67202
(316) 269-6486

U.S. Bankruptcy Court
District of Kansas
500 State Avenue
161 U.S. Courthouse
Kansas City, KS 66101
(913) 551-6732

U.S. Bankruptcy Court
District of Kansas
Carlson Federal Building and U.S. Courthouse
444 S.E. Quincy St, Room 250
Topeka, KS 66683
(913) 295-2750

KENTUCKY

State government information number: (502) 564-3130

Division of Driver Licensing
State Office Building
501 High Street, 2nd Floor
Frankfort, KY 40622
(502) 564-6800

Kentucky Bar Association
514 West Main Street
Frankfort, KY 40601-1883
(502) 564-3795, (502) 564-3225 Fax
http://www.kybar.org

Secretary of State Office
Corporation Division
PO Box 718
Frankfort, KY 40602
(502) 564-7330, (502) 564-4075 Fax

U.S. Bankruptcy Court
Eastern District of Kentucky
PO Box 1111
Lexington, KY 40588-1111
(606) 233-2608

U.S. Bankruptcy Court
Western District of Kentucky
Gene Snyder U.S. Courthouse
601 W. Broadway, Room 546
Louisville, KY 40202-2264
(502) 582-5145

LOUISIANA

State government information number: (504) 342-6600

Louisiana Department of Public Safety
O.D.R.
PO Box 64886
Baton Rouge, LA 70896
(504) 925-6009

Louisiana State Bar Association
601 St. Charles Avenue
New Orleans, LA 70130
(504) 566-1600, (504) 566-0930 Fax

Secretary of State
Corporation Division
PO Box 94125
Baton Rouge, LA 70804-9125
(504) 925-4792
(504) 925-4726 Fax

U.S. Bankruptcy Court
Eastern District of Louisiana
Hale Boggs Federal Bldg, Suite 601
501 Magazine Street
New Orleans, LA 70130
(504) 589-6506

U.S. Bankruptcy Court
Middle District of Louisiana
412 N. 4th Street, Room 301
Baton Rouge, LA 70802
(504) 389-0211

U.S. Bankruptcy Court
Western District of Louisiana
U.S. Courthouse, Suite 2201
300 Fannin Street
Shreveport, LA 71101-3089
(318) 676-4267

U.S. Bankruptcy Court
Western District of Louisiana
300 Jackson Street
Alexandria, LA 71301
(318) 445-1890

U.S. Bankruptcy Court
Western District of Louisiana
205 Federal Building
Union and Vine Streets
Opelousas, LA 70570
(318) 948-3451

MAINE
State government information number: (207) 582-9500

Dept of Motor Vehicles
Driving Records
State House Station 29
August, ME 04333
(207) 287- 2733

Maine State Bar Association
124 State Street
Augusta, ME 04330
(207) 622-7523, (207) 623-0083 Fax
E-mail: info@mainebar.org

Secretary of State
Bureau of Corporations
State House Station 101
Augusta, ME 04333-0101
(207) 287-4190

U.S. Bankruptcy Court
District of Maine
537 Congress Street, 2nd Floor
Portland, ME 04101-3318
(207) 780-3482

U.S. Bankruptcy Court
District of Maine
U.S. Courthouse, Room 311
202 Harlow Street
Bangor, ME 04401
(207) 945-0348

MARYLAND
State government information number: no number listed.

Motor Vehicle Administration
6601 Ritchie Highway
Glen Burnie, MD 21062
(410) 787-7758

Maryland State Bar Association
520 West Fayette Street
Baltimore, MD 21201
(410) 685-7878
(410) 837-0518 Fax
http://www.msba.org

State Department of Assessment and Taxation
Charter Department
301 W. Preston
Baltimore, MD 21201
(410) 225-1330

U.S. Bankruptcy Court
U.S. Courthouse
101 W. Lombard Street
Baltimore, MD 21201
(410) 962-2688, ext. 3038

U.S. Bankruptcy Court
U.S. Courthouse
6500 Cherrywood Lane
Greenbelt, MD 20770
(301) 344-8018

MASSACHUSETTS
State government information number: (617) 727-7030

Registry of Motor Vehicles
Court Records Section
100 Nashua Street
Boston, MA 02114
(617) 727-3842

Massachusetts Bar Association
20 West Street
Boston, MA 02111
(617) 542-3602
(617) 338-0650 Fax

Secretary of State
Corporation Division
1 Ashburton Place
Boston, MA 02108
(617) 727-2850

U.S. Bankruptcy Court
District of Massachusetts
1101 Thomas O'Neill Federal Building
10 Causeway Street
Boston, MA 02222-1074
(617) 565-6050

U.S. Bankruptcy Court
District of Massachusetts
Donohue Federal Building, Room 211
595 Main Street
Worcester, MA 01608-2076
(508) 793-0518

MICHIGAN
State government information number: (517) 373-1837

Department of State
7064 Crowner Drive
Lansing, MI 48918
(517) 322-1618, (517) 322-1181 Fax

State Bar of Michigan
306 Townsend Street
Lansing, MI 48933-2083
(517) 372-9030, (517) 482-6248 Fax
http://www.michbar.org
E-mail: webmeister@michbar.org

Michigan Department of Commerce
Corporation and Securities Bureau
Corporation Division
PO Box 30054
Lansing, MI 48909
(900) 555-0031

U.S. Bankruptcy Court
Eastern District of Michigan
Theodore Levin U.S. Courthouse
231 West Lafayette Boulevard, Room 1004
Detroit, MI 48226
(313) 226-6395

U.S. Bankruptcy Court
Eastern District of Michigan
PO Box X911
Bay City, MI 48707
(517) 894-8840

U.S. Bankruptcy Court
Eastern District of Michigan
226 West Second Street
Flint, MI 48502
(810) 235-4126

U.S. Bankruptcy Court
Western District of Michigan
PO Box 3310
Grand Rapids, MI 49501
(616) 456-2693

U.S. Bankruptcy Court
Western District of Michigan
PO Box 909
Marquette, MI 49855
(906) 226-2117

MINNESOTA
State government information number: (612) 296-6013

Transportation Building
Department of Public Safety
395 John Ireland Blvd., Room 108
St. Paul, MN 55155
(612) 296-2023

Minnesota State Bar Association
514 Nicollet Mall, #300
Minneapolis, MN 55402
(612) 333-1183
(612) 333-4927 Fax

Secretary of State
Business Recording Section
180 State Office Bldg
St. Paul, MN 55155
(612) 297-1455

U.S. Bankruptcy Court
600 Towle Building
330 Second Avenue South
Minneapolis, MN 55401
(612) 348-1855

U.S. Bankruptcy Court
Federal Building and U.S. Courthouse
Room 416
Duluth, MN 55802
(218) 720-5253

U.S. Bankruptcy Court
Warren E. Burger Federal Building
316 North Robert Street
St. Paul, MN 55101
(612) 290-3035

U.S. Bankruptcy Court
205 U.S. Courthouse
118 S. Mill Street
Fergus Falls, MN 56537
(218) 739-4671

MISSISSIPPI
State government information number: (601) 359-1000

Mississippi Highway Patrol
Driver Records
PO Box 958
Jackson, MS 39205
(601) 987-1274

The Mississippi Bar
643 N. State Street
Jackson, MS 39202
(601) 948-4471
(601) 355-8635 Fax
E-mail: msbar@mslawyer.com

Secretary of State
Corporation Division
202 N. Congress Street, Suite 601
Jackson, MS 39201
(601) 359-1633

U.S. Bankruptcy Court
Northern District of Mississippi
205 Federal Building
PO Drawer 867
Aberdeen, MS 39730-0867
(601) 369-2596

U.S. Bankruptcy Court
100 E. Capitol Street
PO Drawer 2448
Jackson, MS 39225-2448
(601) 965-5301

MISSOURI
State government information number: (573) 751-2000

Driver License Bureau
PO Box 200
Jefferson City, MO 65105-0200
(573) 751- 2730

The Missouri Bar
326 Monroe Street
Jefferson City, MO 65102
(573) 635-4128
(573) 635-2811 Fax
http://www.mobar.org

Office of Secretary of State
Corporation Division
600 W. Main Street
PO Box 778
Jefferson City, MO 65102
(573) 751-4153

U.S. Bankruptcy Court
Eastern District of Missouri
211 N. Broadway
St. Louis, MO 63102
(314) 425-4222

U.S. Bankruptcy Court
Western District of Missouri
811 Grand Avenue, Room 913
Kansas City, MO 64106
(816) 426-3321

MONTANA
State government information number: (406) 444-2511

Driver Services
303 N. Roberts
Helena, MT 59620-1420
(406) 444-3275

State Bar of Montana
46 North Last Chance Gulch
Helena, MT 59601
(406) 442-7660
(406) 442-7763 Fax

Secretary of State
Business Services Bureau
State Capitol, Room 225
PO Box 202801
Helena, MT 59620
(406) 444-3665
(406) 444-3976 Fax

U.S. Bankruptcy Court
273 Federal Building
PO Box 689
Butte, MT 59703
(406) 782-3354, (406) 496-3474 Fax

NEBRASKA
State government information number: (402) 471-2311

Department of Motor Vehicles
Driver Record Office
State Office Bldg
Lincoln, NE 68509-4789
(402) 471-3887

Nebraska State Bar Association
625 South 14th, 2nd Floor
Lincoln, NE 68508
(402) 475-7091, (402) 475-7098 Fax
E-mail: nsba01@nol.org

Secretary of State
State Capitol Bldg
Lincoln, NE 68509
(402) 471-4079

U.S. Bankruptcy Court
4600 Federal Building
100 Centennial Mall North
Lincoln, NE 68508
(402) 437-5100

U.S. Bankruptcy Court
215 North 17th Street, Room 8419
PO Box 428, DTS
Omaha, NE 68101-0428
(402) 221-4687, (402) 221-3209 Fax

NEVADA
State government information number: (702) 687-5000

Department of Motor Vehicles &
    Public Safety
Records Section
555 Wright Way
Carson City, NV 89711-0250
(702) 687-5505

State Bar of Nevada
201 Las Vegas Blvd. South
Suite 200
Las Vegas, NV 89101
(702) 382-2200
(702) 385-2878 Fax

Secretary of State
Corporation Division
Capitol Complex
Carson City, NV 89710
(900) 535-3355

U.S. Bankruptcy Court
District of Nevada
Foley Federal Building
300 Las Vegas Blvd, South
Las Vegas, NV 89101
(702) 388-6257

U.S. Bankruptcy Court
District of Nevada
Young Federal Building and U.S. Courthouse
300 Booth Street, Suite 4005
Reno, NV 89509
(702) 784-5559

NEW HAMPSHIRE
State government information number: (603) 271-1110

Director of Motor Vehicle Records
10 Hazen Drive
Concord, NH 03306
(603) 271-2322

New Hampshire Bar Association
112 Pleasant Street
Concord, NH 03301
(603) 224-6942, (603) 224-2910 Fax

Secretary of State
Corporation Division
107 N. Main Street
State House, Room 204
Concord, NH 03301
(603) 271-3246, (603) 271-3244

U.S. Bankruptcy Court
722 Norris Cotton Federal Building
275 Chestnut Street
Manchester, NH 03101
(603) 666-7532

NEW JERSEY
State government information number: (609) 292-2121

Motor Vehicle Services
Bureau of Information Management
Abstract Section, CN 142
Trenton, NJ 08666-0142
(609) 292-4557

New Jersey State Bar Association
One Constitution Square
New Brunswick, NJ 08901-1500
(908) 249-5000, (908) 249-2815 Fax
http://jsba.com

State of New Jersey, Dept of State
Division of Commercial Recording
820 Bear Tavern Rd, 2nd Floor
Tenton, NJ 08628
(609) 530-6400

U.S. Bankruptcy Court
District of New Jersey
King Federal Building & U.S. Courthouse
50 Walnut Street, 3rd Floor
Newark, NJ 07102
(201) 645-3930

U.S. Bankruptcy Court
District of New Jersey
15 North 7th Street
Camden, NJ 08102-1104
(609) 757-5485

U.S. Bankruptcy Court
District of New Jersey
Fisher Federal Building & U.S. Courthouse
402 East State Street
Trenton, NJ 08608
(609) 989-2128

NEW MEXICO
State government information number: (505) 827-4011

Motor Vehicle Division
Driver Services
PO Box 1028
Santa Fe, NM 87604
(505) 827-2234, (505) 827-2267 Fax

State Bar of New Mexico
5121 Masthead, N.E.
Albuquerque, NM 87109
(505) 797-6000
(505) 828-3765 Fax

State Corporation Commission
Corporation Department
PO Drawer 1269
Santa Fe, NM 87504-1269
(505) 827-4504, (505) 827-4509

U.S. Bankruptcy Court
District of New Mexico
PO Box 546
Albuquerque, NM 87103-0546
(505) 248-6500

NEW YORK
State government information number: (518) 474-2121

New York State
Department of Motor Vehicles
Division of Data Preparation
Empire State Plaza
Albany, NY 12228-0430
(518) 474-0841

New York State Bar Association
One Elk Street
Albany, NY 12207
(518) 463-3200, (518) 487-5579 Fax
http://www.nysba.org

Secretary of State
Division of Corporation
162 Washington Avenue
Albany, NY 12231
(518) 473-2492

U.S. Bankruptcy Court
Eastern District of New York
75 Clinton Street
Brooklyn, NY 11201
(718) 330-2188

U.S. Bankruptcy Court
Eastern District of New York
601 Veterans Memorial Highway
Hauppauge, NY 11788
(516) 361-8601

U.S. Bankruptcy Court
Eastern District of New York
1635 Privado Road
Westbury, NY 11590
(516) 832-8801

U.S. Bankruptcy Court
Northern District of New York
James T. Foley U.S. Courthouse
445 Broadway, Room 327
Albany, NY 12207
(518) 431-0188

U.S. Bankruptcy Court
Northern District of New York
Alexander Pirnie Federal Building
Room 230
10 Broad Street
Utica, NY 13501
(315) 793-8101

U.S. Bankruptcy Court
Southern District of New York
Alexander Hamilton Custom House
One Bowling Green, 6th Floor
New York, NY 10004-1408
(212) 688-2870

U.S. Bankruptcy Court
Southern District of New York
176 Church Street
Poughkeepsie, NY 12601
(914) 452-4200

U.S. Bankruptcy Court
Southern District of New York
U.S. Courthouse
300 Quarropas Street
White Plains, NY 10601
(914) 390-4060

U.S. Bankruptcy Court
Western District of New York
68 Court St, 312 U.S. Courthouse
Buffalo, NY 14202
(716) 551-4130

U.S. Bankruptcy Court
Western District of New York
100 State St, 1220 U.S. Courthouse
Rochester, NY 14614
(716) 263-3148

NORTH CAROLINA
State government information number: (919) 733-1110

NC Dept of Transportation
Division of Motor Vehicles
1100 New Bern Avenue
Raleigh, NC 27697-0001
(910) 733-4241

North Carolina State Bar
208 Fayetteville Street Mall
Raleigh, NC 27601
(919) 828-4620, (919) 821-9168 Fax

North Carolina Bar Association
8000 Weston Parkway
Cary, NC 27513
(919) 677-0561, (919) 677-0761 Fax
http://www.barlinc.org

Secretary of State Office
Corporation Division
300 N. Salisbury Street
Raleigh, NC 27603-5909
(910) 733-4201

U.S. Bankruptcy Court
Eastern District of North Carolina
PO Box 1441
Raleigh, NC 27602-1441
(919) 856-4752

U.S. Bankruptcy Court
Eastern District of North Carolina
PO Box 2807
Wilson, NC 27894-2807
(919) 237-0248

U.S. Bankruptcy Court
Middle District of North Carolina
PO Box 26100
Greensboro, NC 27402-6100
(910) 333-5647

U.S. Bankruptcy Court
Western District of North Carolina
Charles R. Jonas Federal Building
401 West Trade Street, Room 209
Charlotte, NC 28202
(704) 344-6103

NORTH DAKOTA
State government information number: (701) 328-2000

Driver License Division Records
608 E. Boulevard Ave.
Bismarck, ND 58505
(701) 328-2600

State Bar Association of North Dakota
515 1/2 East Broadway, Suite 101
Bismarck, ND 58501
(701) 255-1404
(701) 224-1621 Fax

Secretary of State
Corporation Division, State Capitol
600 E. Blvd
Bismarck, ND 58505
(701) 224-4284
(701) 224-2992 Fax

U.S. Bankruptcy Court
District of North Dakota
PO Box 1110
Fargo, ND 58107
(701) 239-5120

OHIO
State government information number: (614) 466-2000

Bureau of Motor Vehicles
ATTN: ABST
PO Box 16520
Columbus, OH 43266-0020
(614) 752-7600

Ohio State Bar Association
1700 Lake Shore Drive
Columbus, OH 43204
(614) 487-2050, (614) 487-1008 Fax

Secretary of State
Corporation Commission
State Office Tower, 14th Floor
Columbus, OH 43266-0418
(614) 466-3910

U.S. Bankruptcy Court
Northern District of Ohio
U.S. Courthouse and Federal Building
2 South Main Street
Akron, OH 44308
(216) 375-5840

U.S. Bankruptcy Court
Northern District of Ohio
201 Cleveland Avenue, S.W.
Frank T. Bow Federal Building
Canton, OH 44702
(216) 489-4426, (216) 489-4434 Fax

U.S. Bankruptcy Court
Northern District of Ohio
Society Center, Suite 3001
Cleveland, OH 44114-1309
(216) 522-4373

U.S. Bankruptcy Court
Northern District of Ohio
411 U.S. Courthouse
1716 Spielbusch Avenue
Toledo, OH 43624
(419) 259-6440

U.S. Bankruptcy Court
Northern District of Ohio
PO Box 147
Youngstown, OH 44501
(216) 746-7027

U.S. Bankruptcy Court
Southern District of Ohio
Atrium Two, Suite 800
221 East Fourth Street
Cincinnati, OH 45202
(513) 684-2572

U.S. Bankruptcy Court
Southern District of Ohio
170 North High Street
Columbus, OH 43215-2403
(614) 469-6638

U.S. Bankruptcy Court
Southern District of Ohio
120 West Third Street
Dayton, OH 45402
(513) 225-2516

OKLAHOMA
State government information number: (405) 521-2011

Department of Public Safety
Driving Records
PO Box 11415
Oklahoma City, OK 73136
(405) 425-2262

Oklahoma Bar Association
1901 North Lincoln
Oklahoma City, OK 73105
(405) 524-2365
(405) 524-1115 Fax

Office of Secretary of State
Corporation Division
101 State Capitol
Oklahoma City, OK 73105
(900) 820-2424

U.S. Bankruptcy Court
Eastern District of Oklahoma
PO Box 1347
Okmulgee, OK 74447
(918) 758-0126

U.S. Bankruptcy Court
Northern District of Oklahoma
224 South Boulder Ave, #105
Tulsa, OK 74103-3015
(918) 581-7181

U.S. Bankruptcy Court
Western District of Oklahoma
Old Post Office Building
215 Dean A. McGee Avenue
Oklahoma City, OK 73102
(405) 231-5642

OREGON
State government information number: no number listed.

Motor Vehicle Division
1905 Lana Avenue, N.E.
Salem, OR 97314
(503) 378-4085

Oregon State Bar
5200 S.W. Meadows Road
Lake Oswego, OR 97035-0889
(503) 620-0222
(503) 684-1366 Fax
http://osbar@osbar.org

Secretary of State
Corporation Division
158 12th Street, N.E.
Salem, OR 97310
(503) 378-4166

U.S. Bankruptcy Court
District of Oregon
1001 S.W. 5th Avenue, Suite 700
Portland, OR 97204
(503) 326-2231

U.S. Bankruptcy Court
District of Oregon
151 West 7th St, Suite 300
Eugene, OR 97401
(503) 465-6448

PENNSYLVANIA
State government information number: (717) 787-2121

Department of Transportation
Bureau of Driver Licensing
PO Box 68695
Harrisburg, PA 17106-8695
(717) 787-3130

Pennsylvania State Bar Association
100 South Street
Harrisburg, PA 17108
(717) 238-6715
(717) 238-1204 Fax
E-mail: pabar@ezonline.com

Department of State
Corporation Bureau
308 N. Office Bldg
Harrisburg, PA 17120
(717) 787-1057

U.S. Bankruptcy Court
Eastern District of Pennsylvania
U.S. Courthouse
601 Market Street, Room 3726
Philadelphia, PA 19106-1797
(215) 597-0926

U.S. Bankruptcy Court
Eastern District of Pennsylvania
Madison Building, Suite 300
400 Washington Street
Reading, PA 19601
(610) 320-5255

U.S. Bankruptcy Court
Middle District of Pennsylvania
PO Box 908
Harrisburg, PA 17108
(717) 782-2260

U.S. Bankruptcy Court
Middle District of Pennsylvania
217 Federal Building
197 South Main Street
Wilkes-Barre, PA 18701
(717) 826-6450

U.S. Bankruptcy Court
Western District of Pennsylvania
Federal Building
1000 Liberty Ave, Room 1602
Pittsburgh, PA 15222
(412) 644-2700

U.S. Bankruptcy Court
Western District of Pennsylvania
PO Box 1755
Erie, PA 16507
(814) 453-7580

RHODE ISLAND
State government information number: (401) 277-2000

Division of Motor Vehicles
Room 212
345 Harris Avenue
Providence, RI 02909
(401) 277-2994

Rhode Island Bar Association
115 Cedar Street
Providence, RI 02903
(401) 421-5740, (401) 421-2703 Fax
http://www.ribar.com

Department of State
Corporations Division
100 N. Main Street
Providence, RI 02903
(401) 277-2357

U.S. Bankruptcy Court
District of Rhode Island
The Federal Center
380 Westminster Mall
Providence, RI 02903
(401) 528-4477

SOUTH CAROLINA
State government information number: (803) 734-1000

South Carolina Department of Public Safety
Motor Vehicle Division
PO Box 1498
Columbia, SC 29216-0030
(803) 251-2940

South Carolina Bar
950 Taylor Street
Columbia, SC 29202
(803) 799-6653, (803) 799-4118 Fax
http://www.scar.org

Dept of State, Corporation Division
Box 11350
Columbia, SC 29211
(803) 734-2158, (803) 734-2164 Fax

U.S. Bankruptcy Court
PO Box 1448
Columbia, SC 29202
(803) 765-5436

SOUTH DAKOTA
State government information number: (605) 773-3011

Department of Commerce
Drive License Issuance
118 W. Capitol
Pierre, SD 57501
(605) 773-4127

State Bar of South Dakota
222 East Capitol
Pierre, SD 57501
(605) 224-7554
(605) 224-0282 Fax
http://sdbar.org

Secretary of State
Corporation Commission
500 E. Capitol
Pierre, SD 57510
(605) 773-4854

U.S. Bankruptcy Court
District of South Dakota
225 S. Pierre, Room 203
Pierre, SD 57501
(605) 224-6013

U.S. Bankruptcy Court
District of South Dakota
PO Box 5060
Sioux Falls, SD 57117-5060
(605) 330-4541

TENNESSEE
State government information number: (615) 741-3011

Tennessee Department of Safety
1150 Foster Avenue
Nashville, TN 37249-4000
(615) 741-3954

Tennessee Bar Association
3622 West End Avenue
Nashville, TN 37205
(615) 383-7421
(615) 297-8058 Fax
http://www.tba.org

Division of Services
ATTN: Certification
Suite 1800
James K. Polk Bldg
Nashville, TN 37243-0306
(615) 741-2816

U.S. Bankruptcy Court
Eastern District of Tennessee
Historic U.S. Courthouse
31 East 11th Street
Chattanooga, TN 37402-2722
(423) 752-5163

U.S. Bankruptcy Court
Eastern District of Tennessee
First Tennessee Plaza, Suite 1501
Knoxville, TN 37929-1501
(423) 545-4279

U.S. Bankruptcy Court
Middle District of Tennessee
701 Broadway
207 Customs House
Nashville, TN 37203
(615) 736-5590

U.S. Bankruptcy Court
Western District of Tennessee
Federal Building
109 South Highland Ave, #308
Jackson, TN 38301
(901) 424-9751

U.S. Bankruptcy Court
Western District of Tennessee
One Memphis Place
200 Jefferson Avenue, Suite 413
Memphis, TN 38103-2328
(901) 544-3202

TEXAS
State government information number: (512) 463-4630

Texas Department of Public Safety
ATTN: LIDR
PO Box 15999
Austin, TX 78761-5999
(512) 465-2000

State Bar of Texas
1414 Colorado
Austin, TX 78701-1627
(512) 463-1463, (512) 463-1475 Fax

Secretary of State
Corporation Division
PO Box 13697
Austin, TX 78711
(512) 463-5555, (512) 463-5709 Fax

U.S. Bankruptcy Court
Eastern District of Texas
Brooks Federal Building and U.S. Courthouse
300 Willow Street, Suite 100
Beaumont, TX 77701
(409) 839-2617

U.S. Bankruptcy Court
Eastern District of Texas
200 East Ferguson Street
Second Floor
Tyler, TX 75702
(903) 592-1212

U.S. Bankruptcy Court
Northern District of Texas
PO Box 15960
Amarillo, TX 79105-0960
(806) 376-2302

U.S. Bankruptcy Court
Northern District of Texas
Cabell Federal Building and U.S. Courthouse
1100 Commerce Street, Room 12A24
Dallas, TX 75242-1496
(214) 767-0814

U.S. Bankruptcy Court
Northern District of Texas
501 West 10th Street
206 U.S. Courthouse
Ft. Worth, TX 76102-3643
(817) 334-3802

U.S. Bankruptcy Court
Northern District of Texas
Mahon Federal Building and U.S. Courthouse
1205 Texas Avenue
Room 102
Lubbock, TX 79401-4002
(806) 743-7336

U.S. Bankruptcy Court
Southern District of Texas
615 Leopard Street, Suite 113
Corpus Christi, TX 78476
(512) 888-3484

U.S. Bankruptcy Court
Southern District of Texas
PO Box 61010
Houston, TX 77208
(713) 250-5115

U.S. Bankruptcy Court
Western District of Texas
816 Congress Avenue, Suite 1420
Austin, TX 78701
(512) 916-5238

U.S. Bankruptcy Court
Western District of Texas
8515 Lockheed Drive
El Paso, TX 79925
(915) 779-7362

U.S. Bankruptcy Court
Western District of Texas
U.S. Post Office Annex, Rm P-163
Midland, TX 79701
(915) 683-1650

U.S. Bankruptcy Court
Western District of Texas
PO Box 1439
San Antonio, TX 78295-1439
(210) 229-5187

U.S. Bankruptcy Court
Western District of Texas
St. Charles Place, Suite 20
600 Austin Avenue
Waco, TX 76701
(817) 754-1481

UTAH
State government information number: (801) 538-3000

Driver License Division
ATTN: Public Assistance Section
4501 South 2700 West, 3rd Floor
PO Box 30560
Salt Lake City, UT 84130-0560
(801) 965-4437, (801) 965-4496 Fax

Utah State Bar
645 South 200 East, Suite 310
Salt Lake City, UT 84111
(801) 531-9077, (801) 531-0660 Fax
http://www.utahbar.org

Department of Commerce
Utah Division of Corporation
PO Box 45801
Salt Lake City, UT 84145-0801
(801) 530-4849

U.S. Bankruptcy Court
District of Utah
Frank E. Moss U.S. Courthouse
350 South Main Street, Room 361
Salt Lake City, UT 84101
(801) 524-5157

VERMONT
State government information number: (802) 828-1110

Department of Motor Vehicles
Driver Improvement
120 State Street
Montpelier, VT 05603
(802) 828-2050

Vermont Bar Association
PO Box 100
Montpelier, VT 05601-0100
(802) 223-2020, (802) 223-1573 Fax
http://www.vtbar.org

Secretary of State
Corporation Division
109 State Street
Montpelier, VT 05609-1102
(802) 828-2386

U.S. Bankruptcy Court
District of Vermont
PO Box 6648
Rutland, VT 05702-6648
(802) 747-7625

VIRGINIA

State government information number: (804) 786-0000

Department of Motor Vehicles
Information Department
PO Box 27412
Richmond, VA 23269
(804) 367-0538

Virginia State Bar
707 East Main Street, Suite 1500
Richmond, VA 23219-2803
(804) 775-0500
(804) 775-0501 Fax
http://www.vsb.org

Virginia Bar Association
701 East Franklin, Suite 1120
Richmond, VA 23219
(804) 644-0041
(804) 644-0052 Fax

State Corporation Commission
Tyler Bldg, 1st Floor
1300 E. Main Street
Richmond, VA 23219
(804) 371-9733

U.S. Bankruptcy Court
Eastern District of Virginia
PO Box 19247
Alexandria, VA 22320-0247
(703) 557-1716

U.S. Bankruptcy Court
Eastern District of Virginia
PO Box 120067
Newport News, VA 23612-0067
(804) 595-9805

U.S. Bankruptcy Court
Eastern District of Virginia
PO Box 1938
Norfolk, VA 23501-1938
(804) 441-6651

U.S. Bankruptcy Court
Eastern District of Virginia
U.S. Courthouse Annex, Suite 301
1100 East Main Street
Richmond, VA 23219-3528
(804) 771-2878, ext. 34

U.S. Bankruptcy Court
Western District of Virginia
PO Box 1407
Harrisonburg, VA 22801
(540) 434-8327

U.S. Bankruptcy Court
Western District of Virginia
PO Box 2390
Roanoke, VA 24010
(540) 857-2391

WASHINGTON
State government information number: (360) 753-5000

Dept of Licensing, Driving Records
PO Box 9030
Olympia, WA 98507
(206) 753-6960

Washington State Bar Association
500 Westin Building
2001 Sixth Avenue
Seattle, WA 98121-2599
(206) 727-8200, (206) 727-8320 Fax
http://www.wsba.org

Secretary of State
Corporation Division
Republic Bldg, 2nd Floor
PO Box 40234
Olympia, WA 98504-0234
(206) 753-7115, (206) 753-7120

U.S. Bankruptcy Court
Eastern District of Washington
PO Box 2164
Spokane, WA 99201
(509) 353-2404

U.S.Bankruptcy Court
Western District of Washington
Park Place Bldg,
1200 6th Avenue, Suite 315
Seattle, WA 98101
(206) 553-7545

U.S. Bankruptcy Court
Western District of Washington
1717 Pacific Avenue, Room 2100
Tacoma, WA 98402-3233
(206) 593-6310

WEST VIRGINIA
State government information number: (304) 558-3456

Division of Motor Vehicles
Driving Records
1900 Kanawha Blvd. E
Charleston, WV 25317
(304) 348-0238

West Virginia State Bar
2006 Kanawha Blvd, East
Charleston, WV 25311
(304) 558-2456
(304) 558-2467 Fax
http://www.wvbar.org

West Virginia Bar Association
PO Box 3956
Charleston, WV 25339
(304) 895-3663 Phone/Fax

Secretary of State
Corporation Division
State Capitol
Charleston, WV 25305
(304) 558-8000

U.S. Bankruptcy Court
Northern District of West Virginia
PO Box 70
Wheeling, WV 26003
(304) 233-1655

U.S. Bankruptcy Court
Southern District of West Virginia
500 Quarrier Street
2210 Federal Building
Charleston, WV 25301
(304) 347-5114

WISCONSIN
State government information number: (608) 266-2211

Wisconsin Department of Transportation
Driver Record Files
PO Box 7918
Madison, WI 53707-7918
(608) 266-2353

State Bar of Wisconsin
402 West Wilson Street
Madison, WI 53703
(608) 257-3838, (608) 257-5502 Fax
http://www.wisbar.org

Office of Secretary of State
Corporation Division
PO Box 7846
Madison, WI 53707-7846
(608) 266-3590

U.S. BankruptcyCourt
Eastern District of Wisconsin
517 E. Wisconsin Avenue
126 U.S. Courthouse
Milwaukee, WI 53202
(414) 297-3293

U.S. Bankruptcy Court
Western District of Wisconsin
PO Box 5009
Eau Claire, WI 54702-5009
(715) 839-2980

U.S. Bankruptcy Court
Western District of Wisconsin
PO Box 548
Madison, WI 53701
(608) 264-5178

WYOMING
State government information number: (307) 777-7011

Wyoming Department of Transportation
Driving Services
PO Box 1708
Cheyenne, WY 82002
(307) 777-4800

Wyoming State Bar
500 Randall Avenue
Cheyenne, WY 82001
(307) 632-9061
(307) 632-3737 Fax

Wyoming Secretary of State
Corporation Division
The Capitol
Cheyenne, WY 82002
(307) 777-7311

U.S. Bankruptcy Court
District of Wyoming
PO Box 1107
Cheyenne, WY 82003
(307) 772-2191

Appendix C

☑ *Federal Government Sources*

The Federal Aviation Administration

The Federal Aviation Administration will provide a pilot's current address. It's possible for the FAA to search with a name only, if it's a unique name. If the name is common, more information is necessary, such as: date of birth, Social Security number, or an FAA pilot certificate number.

FAA/Aircraft Registry
6425 S. Denning
PO Box 25504
Oklahoma City, OK 73125
(405) 954-3261

FAA/Airmen Certification
AVN 460
PO Box 25082
Oklahoma City, OK 73125
(405) 954-3261

American Bar Association

American Bar Association
750 North Lake Shore Drive
Chicago, IL 60611
(312) 988-6281
http://www.abanet.org/

Federal Courts

There is at least one U.S. District and one U.S. Bankruptcy Court in each state. Most larger states have many courts. *The Sourcebook of Federal Courts, U.S. District and Bankruptcy* by BRB Publications, and the *United States Court Directory,* available from the Government Printing Office (see below), are two books that list U.S. courts. You may also contact the Federal Information Center for a specific court's address (see below).

Federal Information Center

This is an excellent resource for obtaining information or locations of federal agencies (executive branch, congressional offices, and federal courts). They will assist in providing the official name of an agency, or one having jurisdiction over a particular subject or area. Phone (800) 688-9889.

Publications That Can Help

The U.S. Government Printing Office sells numerous books published by the federal government—many that are valuable to searchers. Some include:

U.S. Government Organization Manual lists the address, phone number and description of each federal agency and office.

Directory of U.S. Government Depository Libraries lists libraries that have federal publications.

Where to Write for Vital Records gives details on how to obtain birth, death, marriage and divorce records from each state.

Superintendent of Documents
U.S. Government Printing Office
Washington, DC 20402
(202) 512-1800

The National Zip Code Directory is for sale at any post office. Your library should also have a copy. It lists all cities in the U.S. with a post office, their zip codes, and the county. Streets are listed for larger cities.

National Archives and Records Administration

The National Archives and Records Administration (NARA) is part of the executive branch of the Federal government and is responsible for the maintenance and holdings of all Federal government agency records. As of January, 1997, the National Archives and the Federal Records Centers are both run by NARA. However, separate documents and information are still maintained. The Federal Record Centers maintain documents from federal agencies in their area. You must, however, contact the particular agency that generated (and still owns) the records to get permission to view them. The agency will also give you a bunch of numbers that indicate the exact location of their file at the Federal Records Center. After 25 years or so, the records are turned over to the archives section. The NARA website explains what is held where (www.nara.com).

NARA National Offices

National Archives and Records Administration
Seventh & Pennsylvania Ave NW
Washington, DC 20408
(202) 501-5400
Records: National

National Archives and Records Administration
8601 Adelphi Rd
College Park, MD 20740-6001
(301) 713-6800
Records: National

National Archives and Records Administration
4205 Suitland Road (mail)
Washington, DC 20409-0002
(301) 457-7000
E-mail: center@suitland.nara.gov
Records: National but not open to public.

National Personnel Records Center
Military Records Facility
9700 Page Avenue
St. Louis, MO 63132-5100
U.S. Military records.

National Personnel Records Center
Civilian Records Facility
111 Winnebago Street
St. Louis, MO 63118-4199
Civil service records.

All of the National Archives Regional Centers have the 1920 census (and prior), Revolutionary War records, federal court documents (for their area), and various other historical and genealogical records (for their area). Unlike the state historical/ genealogical societies, the National Archives will not perform searches. You can visit their locations and search their records yourself or contact the Archives for a list of researchers. Local researchers usually charge an hourly fee.

National Archives and Federal Record Centers

National Archives, Northeast Region
100 Dan Fox Drive
Pittsfield, MA 01201-8230
(413) 445-6885
E-mail: archives@pittsfield.nara.gov
Microfilm only. Connecticut, Maine, Massachusetts, New Hampshire, Rhode Island, Vermont.

National Archives, Northeast Region
380 Trapelo Road
Waltham, MA 02154
(617) 647-8100
E-mail: archives@walhtam.nara.gov
Same states as above.

Federal Records Center
Frederick Murphy Federal Center
380 Trapelo Road
Waltham, MA 02154
(617) 647-8104
E-mail: center@waltham.nara.gov

National Archives, Northeast Region
201 Varick Street
New York, NY 10014
(212) 337-1300
E-mail: archives@newyork.nara.gov
New Jersey, New York, Puerto Rico, Virgin Islands.

Federal Records Center
Military Ocean Terminal
Building 22
Bayonne, NJ 07002-5388
(201) 823-7241
E-mail: center@bayonne.nara.gov

National Archives, Mid-Atlantic Region
Ninth & Market Streets
Philadelphia, PA 19107
(215) 597-3000
E-mail: archives@philarch.nara.gov
Delaware, Maryland, Pennsylvania, Virginia, West Virginia.

Federal Records Center
14700 Townsend Road
Philadelphia, PA 19154
(215) 671-9027
E-mail: center@philadelphia.nara.gov

National Archives, Southeast Region
1557 St. Joseph Avenue
East Point, GA 30344-2593
(404) 763-7477
E-mail: archives@atlanta.nara.gov
Alabama, Florida, Georgia, Kentucky, Mississippi, North Carolina, South Carolina, Tennessee.

Federal Records Center
1557 St. Joseph Avenue
East Point, GA 30344-2593
(404) 763-7474
E-mail: center@atlanta.nara.gov

Dayton Federal Records Center
3150 Springboro Road
Dayton, OH 45439
(513) 225-2852

National Archives, Great Lakes Region
7358 South Pulaski Road
Chicago, IL 60629
(773) 581-7816
E-mail: archives@chicago.nara.gov
Illinois, Indiana, Michigan, Minnesota, Ohio,Wisconsin.

Federal Records Center
7358 South Pulaski Rd
Chicago, IL 60629
(773) 581-7816
E-mail: center@chicago.nara.gov

National Archives, Central Plains Region
2312 East Bannister Road
Kansas City, MO 64131
(816) 926-6982
E-mail: archives@kansascity.nara.gov
Iowa, Kansas, Minnesota, Missouri, Nebraska, North Dakota, South Dakota.

Federal Records Center
2312 East Bannister Road
Kansas City, MO 64131
(816) 926-7272

National Archives, Southwest Region
501 West Felix Street, Bldg 1, Dock 1
PO Box 6216
Ft. Worth, TX 76115-0216
(817) 334-5525
E-mail: archives@ftworth.nara.gov
Arkansas, Louisiana, Oklahoma, Texas.

Federal Records Center
501 West Felix Street, Bldg 1, Dock 1
PO Box 6216
Ft. Worth, TX 76115-0216
(817) 334-5515
E-mail: center@ftworth.nara.gov

National Archives, Rocky Mountain Region
Denver Federal Center, Bldg 48
PO Box 25307
Denver, CO 80225
(303) 236-0817
E-mail: archives@denver.nara.gov
Colorado, Montana, New Mexico, North Dakota, South Dakota, Utah, Wyoming.

Federal Records Center
Denver Federal Center, Bldg 48
PO Box 25307
Denver, CO 80225
(303) 236-0804
E-mail: center@denver.nara.gov

National Archives, Pacific Region
24000 Avila Road
Laguna Niguel, CA 92677
(714) 360-2641
E-mail: archives@laguna.nara.gov
Arizona, Southern California, Nevada (Clark County).

Federal Records Center
24000 Avila Road, 1st Floor
PO Box 6719
Laguna Niguel, CA 92677-6719
(714) 360-2626
E-mail: lagunafrc@laguna.nara.gov

National Archives, Pacific Region
1000 Commodore Drive
San Bruno, CA 94066
(415) 876-9009
E-mail: archives@sanbruno.nara.gov
California, Hawaii, Nevada (except Clark County), American Samoa, Guam, Trust Territory of Pacific Islands.

Federal Records Center
1000 Commodore Drive
San Bruno, CA 94066
(415) 876-9001
E-mail: center@sanbruno.nara.gov

National Archives, Pacific Alaska Region
6125 Sand Point Way, NE
Seattle, WA 98115
(206) 526-6507
E-mail: archives@seattle.nara.gov
Idaho, Oregon, Washington.

Federal Records Center
6125 Sand Point Way, NE
Seattle, WA 98115
(206) 526-6501

National Archives, Pacific Alaska Region
654 West Third Avenue
Anchorage, AK 99501-2145
(907) 271-2441
E-mail: archives@alaska.nara.gov
Alaska.

About the Author

Don Ray is a multi-media investigative reporter/producer/author based out of Burbank, California. He is noted as one of the country's leading experts in finding people and information. He has produced national investigative stories for "Inside Edition" and "The Crusaders." He also worked for the NBC and CBS television stations in Los Angeles and the Public Broadcasting System's station in Phoenix. He has won awards for investigative reporting and news writing. He is the reporter who first broke the story of the child molestation investigation of singer Michael Jackson.

Don is the author of *California's Investigators Handbook*, now in its sixth edition. He has written numerous magazine and newspapers articles across the world. Don ran his own investigative news service in southern California and taught investigative reporting and TV news writing at UCLA Extension.

Don is also a sought-after public speaker. Over the past decade, the 48-year-old California native has spoken to thousands of journalists, law enforcement investigators, private investigators, genealogists, paralegals and attorneys. He has appeared on numerous national and local television and radio programs and has been featured in a variety of newspapers and magazines.

Bookstore

How to Investigate by Computer, Book II by Ralph D. Thomas. This manual of the new investigative technology gives sources and teaches to investigate by computer. Learn about hard-to-find sources of information and how to access them using a computer. 130 pages, $34.95.

How to Locate Anyone Who Is or Has Been in the Military: *Armed Forces Locator Guide* (7th Edition) by Lt. Col. Richard S. Johnson (Ret). Learn all conceivable means of locating current and former members of the Air Force, Army, Coast Guard, Marine Corps, Navy, Reserve and National Guard. New chapters in this updated and expanded edition include: Verifying Military Service, Locating Women Veterans, and Case Studies. 274 pages, $19.95.

Secrets of Finding Unclaimed Money by Richard S. Johnson. An experienced heir searcher reveals all the secrets of finding unclaimed money held by State Unclaimed Property Offices, other state agencies and the federal government. He also teaches how to earn money by becoming a professional heir searcher. Includes sample forms and contracts. 182 pages, $11.95.

Find Anyone Fast (2nd edition) by Richard S. Johnson and Debra Johnson Knox. Father-daughter private investigators explain how easy it is to find relatives, old romances, military buddies, dead-beat parents, or just about anyone. New chapter includes finding people using the Internet. 256 pages, $16.95.

Please add $4.05 shipping/handling to all orders. Send to:

MIE Publishing
PO Box 17118
Spartanburg, SC 29301
(800) 937-2133, (864) 595-0813 Fax
E-mail: miepub@aol.com

Index